Issues in Women's Rights to Land in Cameroon

Edited by
Lotsmart N. Fonjong

Langaa Research & Publishing CIG
Mankon, Bamenda

Publisher

Langaa RPCIG
Langaa Research & Publishing Common Initiative Group
P.O. Box 902 Mankon
Bamenda
North West Region
Cameroon
Langaagrp@gmail.com
www.langaa-rpcig.net

Distributed in and outside N. America by African Books Collective
orders@africanbookscollective.com
www.africanbookcollective.com

ISBN: 9956-726-83-4

DISCLAIMER
All views expressed in this publication are those of the author and do not necessarily reflect the views of Langaa RPCIG.

Table of Contents

Acknowledgements

Working on a book of this nature with authors from different professional backgrounds and locations can be very demanding. These same factors almost thwarted the book but for the constant encouragement and support from many people who have helped to make this book possible. We are indebted to the Canadian based International Development Research Centre (IDRC) that provided our entire funding and Ms Ramata Thioune of IDRC West Africa Office in Darker who keep reminding me of her desire to read the book.

I want to appreciate the collaboration of Florence Awasom, Harmony Bobga, Michael Yanou, Patience Sone and Vera Ngassa for braving all the odds to turn in their final papers within the deadlines. Many thanks go to Professors Emmanuel Nebasina Ngwa and Galega Samagena who respectively accepted to write the introduction and forward to the book and delivered the job in record time.

Finally, I want to extend special thanks to my colleagues Irene Sama-Lang and Lawrence Fombe of the IDRC-UB Land Rights research team for their contributions and support; the reviewers who worked closely with us to review the papers and the proofreader, Anastasia Smith, of the University of North Carolina Greensboro.

Foreword

It is befitting at this time, to dedicate an entire volume to *Issues in Women's Rights to Land in Cameroon*, as the title of the book announces. As I have observed elsewhere, the concept of equality between the sexes and human dignity everywhere, irrespective of race, is gaining ground in modern democratic thought. The unexplained paradox that persists, however, is why there is ostensibly less vehemence in the condemnation of gender-based discrimination than in the case of racial discrimination, although both characteristics (i.e. race and gender) are by themselves fashioned by the whims of fortune.

The nexus between the reluctance to recognize and materialize women's right to land, and the increasingly visible trend in the feminization of poverty both in the urban and rural milieu, is undeniable. The problem assumes special acuity given that land remains an important factor of production in an essentially agrarian society such as Cameroon. What is even more baffling is that the law as primary regulator of conduct and circumstance in society, i.e. the instrument of justice, has stood by idly in the statute books while discrimination manifested by depriving women of their land rights, continue to be legion. In contemporary Cameroon, the problem is not so much the law as its manner of application. That is why the chapters of this book that have delved into investigating the principal sources and reasons for this prevalent injustice are particularly welcome.

As some of the analyses reveal, denying women their right to land acquisition or inheritance is sometimes contrary to established judicial precedents and even in total dissonance with the country's constitution. Traditional and cultural shibboleths associated with land acquisition and ownership that tend to stymie women's development and fulfilment, must be quickly shirked, for such retrograde excuses can no longer find comfort in the law, morality nor in "modern" traditional thinking. The trend, albeit timid, of appointing women to Land Consultative Boards and even as traditional authorities, can only be salutary. These are some positive practical steps that can translate the notion of equal rights into "equal power" over land for both sexes; otherwise "equality" in this context will remain an unattractive slogan.

Far from being a complete compendium on all questions regarding women's right to land, the book has nevertheless attempted to cover, from varied angles, a range of important issues pertaining to women's right (or the lack thereof) over land. From barebones philosophical perspectives such as the concept of "power and rights", through the legal, economic and social standpoint, the book treats this topical question from a multi-dimensional perspective, and does it well. The varied backgrounds of the contributors give it special flavour – university lecturers of diverse academic disciplines and those involved in the daily application of the law (judges and legal practitioners).The result is an insightful theoretical analysis tempered by a refreshing blend of practical narratives. The reader will also be pleased to learn some of the lessons of comparative experience from abroad (South Africa and Uganda).

The language is generally easy to understand and the chapters provide a rich list of references at the end, which could serve as a useful source for other works on the subject. I will readily recommend this book as a useful source of information to all those interested in reversing gender inequality and women's land rights in particular.

Professor GALEGA Samgena
Head of Department of Law (English)
University of Douala, Cameroon.
Email: galega.samgena@yahoo.com

Summary

Land rights in Africa are governed by legal pluralism animated by statutory, customary, and Islamic laws which, instead of complementing each other, tend to contradict, particularly in the management, acquisition, ownership and disposal of a piece of land. In Cameroon, land rights are regulated by statute, customs and informal arrangements which follow this trend. While the statutory laws informed by the 1996 Constitution, the 1974 Land Ordinances and the subsequent ministerial circulars are gender neutral, customary practices driven by patriarchy are gender biased and discriminate against women. The principle that statutory laws automatically take precedent over any other law in cases where there is conflict between laws seems to remain on paper here. In fact, when it comes to land, informal and customary arrangements dominate and custom is seen to be powerful, authoritative and even unshakable! Very few people, especially in the rural areas, are aware of land statutes and thus do not care to officially register land acquired through customary means.

One of the arguments for this entrenched gender bias that has continued for decades seems to be that we live in a 'man's world' where patriarchy inherent in most customs can often directly influence the process of making and implementing laws and policies. In this case, land laws and policies that are intended to be gender neutral unfortunately end up discriminating against women during implementation. This implies that without major policy and practical reforms that are consciously directed towards women, the predicament of women is unavoidable because they live in a society in which custom is gender discriminatory. It is therefore difficult for gender neutral laws to ensure gender equality in such an environment no matter the good intention of the laws or policies. This is what this book is all about.

Issues in Women's Rights to Land in Cameroon explores the customary, social, economic, political and rights issues surrounding access, ownership and control over land from a gender perspective. It combines theory and practice from researchers, lawyers and judges each with tracked records of working on women's and/or rights concerns to identify and analyse these issues from a multidisciplinary and multi-country perspectives. The outcome of these analyses have been reduced into eight chapters, which will appeal to students, researchers, activists, policy makers, and ordinary readers in any field, but particularly those in the field of Gender, Geography, Law, Political Science, Sociology, and other Social Sciences. The uniqueness of the book is found in the fact that the various contributors have approached gender and rights issues surrounding land tenure from diverse perspectives while, at the same time, maintaining a central focus. In so doing, the contributors have not only been able to diagnose and analyze the problem, but they have also proposed solutions based on critical conclusions. Each chapter introduces something new while also adding more clarity to the debate on gender issues in land rights.

Ngwa's introduction to the book conceptualizes the question of land from where the various authors have been inspired. It is an in-depth overture that relates the issue of women's land rights to customs, agricultural sustainability, natural resources and biodiversity conservation, decentralization, and space management. The author highlights the context of the book in this introductory chapter by framing the question of women's land rights in a global context. He holds that globalization and liberalization have come along with many opportunities for investments in land and security of tenure which enable women to either be a part or to be losers of the global trend. Land ownership therefore is not only about rights but also about power and control as Fonjong sustain.

Fonjong's paper discusses the concept of power and equality in order to demonstrate that gender equality over land as provided by the law does not necessary translate to equal land rights for men and women in the field because of patriarchy, which gives men enormous power over resources. Land laws and policies should therefore be designed and implemented from the premise that the playground is not level for men and women. Even though customs may play a significant role in the current discrimination against women, the solution to discrimination is more than just instituting land reforms. It should rather include regular capacity building in mainstreaming gender for top level management and legislators, and increased sensitization in all facets of the society. This action, according to the author is purely political and thus requires a political will from those in power.

Since power goes with control, men have benefited from endrocentric customs that control both women and resources. That is why Ngassa thinks that the real issue within women's rights to land rotates around the custom of bride-price as construed by the various ethnic communities in Cameroon. In the first paper on women's inheritance, she introduces her central argument that, in customary societies, bride-price defines marriage, childbirth, paternity, widowhood and property. This premise tends to nullify the intended impact of the unprecedented post-colonial human rights laws that try to protect women by redefining marriage, paternity, bride-price and widowhood. She thus concludes that gender discrimination in land ownership will remain an issue as long as obnoxious customs are not modified, changed or discarded. She sustains this argument in her second paper on bride-price by maintaining that bride-price impacts the dissolution of marriage, widowhood, the practice of levirate marriages, and ownership of property, and by advocating that the practice be revisited. But changes that can bring about gender equality require looking beyond the borders for inspirations from others countries like South Africa and Uganda, which have both recently undergone land reforms.

It is in this light that Yanou and Sone approach women's land rights issues from a spatial comparative viewpoint. After tracing the violation of women's land rights to the undue dominant role of traditional authorities (who are naturally committed to adhering to customs) in the Land Consultative Board, the authors go on to demonstrate the similarities between land discrimination in South Africa and in Cameroon. They hold that Section 5 of the South African Glen Gray Act was used to stop Africans whose lands had been dispossessed during Apartheid from trying to regain it through any form of rebellion. In a like manner, Section 12 of Decree No 76/166 of April 1976 in Cameroon is used to protect customary rules and to give a strong voice to traditional representation in the Land Board in order to restrict women's rights to own property. In settling on the fact that there was no substantial differences between rights violated by the land laws in both countries, the authors, however, acknowledge that while in South Africa race was the basis of exclusion during Apartheid, sex is the basis of discrimination in Cameroon.

Fombe and Sama-Lang continue in this same line of argument to interrogate the situation of land reforms in Uganda and South Africa from which to draw possible lessons for Cameroon. They focus on the merits of the land reforms in the two countries in order to illustrate how similar practices can positively impact women's right to land and to ensure empowerment and sustainable livelihood.

Similar to, Yanou and Sone who are very concerned with the power of traditional authorities in land matters in the abuse of women's land rights in Cameroon, Awasom introduces administrative authorities as another group for concern. The author focuses on the statutory stance for women's rights to land vis-à-vis the contradictions from customary laws. She uses this position of land statutes and the distinctions among land ownership, land disposition, land possessions, and land ownership to build a solid case for women's rights. She uses examples of administrative rulings on land litigations which consistently disfavored women simply because they are women to portray evidence of conspiracy between traditional and administrative authorities to protect patriarchy. The land ordinances and administrative practices do not promote gender equality, but rather inequality and they further polarize upper and lower class women in the search for security of tenure. Increasing women's representation in the Land Consultative Board and embarking on extensive rural mobilization and sensitization on women's rights to own land is a possible way forward, the paper concludes.

While acknowledging the weaknesses of the current Cameroon land legislations in the protection of women's inheritance rights, Bobga believes strongly that the solution of the problem lies in affecting profound changes in the legislation. This change, just as Fombe and Sama-Lang reported in the case of Uganda, must be catalyzed by the civil society organizations. Bobga thus argue for strong local human rights NGOs in Cameroon. But as reported in the literature on Cameroonian NGOs, he regretted that many of these NGOs lack both an identity and the required substance to push a government to affect legislative change.

It is obvious that this book does not cover all the questions related to women's land rights in Cameroon but it has attained the objective it set forth for itself in a comprehensive manner—the objective to raise the debate for gender inclusive land reforms in Cameroon while proposing a possible road map that will make Cameroon a more just and prosperous nation where men and women together work as development agencies. It has also highlighted the question of conscience to stakeholders including legislators, judges, administrative and traditional authorities, who, in their individual spheres, have the roles of protecting human rights, including the rights of women. The debate is on and the question is whether obnoxious customary practices and the plethoric land laws, some of which were designed more than forty years ago for a country just acceding to independency within a one party era, can still be relevant for the Cameroon of today.

Lotsmart N. Fonjong
Buea, 2012

Introduction to Land and Rural Women in Cameroon

Nebasina Emmanuel Ngwa

Introduction

In Cameroon, the fact is that absolute rights on a parcel of land reveal an individual's status within his community. Land thus carries along with it a symbol of authority, easy and /or difficult relations with other people in the community. Land is wealth, since on it are embedded the other production assets. Land, especially in rural Cameroon is the traditional and/ or customary seat from which most family decisions and consequently developmental issues take root. Land in rural Cameroon, where within the backdrop of rapid population growth, economic, political liberalization and the institution of private property rights has become, and is likely to remain a scarce resource, which all components of the Cameroonian society want to grab and use. Central to this element of grabbing to use, in a region where there are no industries, no large agro-businesses, but where there is high unemployment and increasing poverty, is that of women's rights over this scarce resource-land. Simply put, there is insecurity of land tenure for women in rural Cameroon.

Current conversations involving gender and women in land tenure matters in Cameroon tend to emphasize the facts of unequal gender power relations which further reduce women's socio-economic development. What then follows is that the social and cultural traditions as well as other societal inbuilt structures of domination and discrimination against women only make such women, especially the less educated, to have very limited property rights over land.

1

With this in mind, and within the scope of this publication, it becomes imperative to examine some of these gender-power relationships so as to propose a way forward. The themes discussed are centered on issues of Equal rights and Unequal power over land, including: Women's inheritance rights in Anglophone Cameroon; The impact of women's Land rights on Empowerment of the Cameroonian woman; The role of civil society in advocating for women's land rights in Cameroon; Women and land registration in Anglophone Cameroon; Women and Land in agricultural development and social stability; Women and land in natural resource and holistic environmental management. There is also Women and land tenure in a patrilineal and matrilineal society, and a host of other themes that do not exclude gateways that open up into a precise road map on how women in Cameroon can register and obtain land certificates. These are the themes and issues that are explored and analyzed by a cross section of experts, each in their field of performance.

Therefore, in this publication, the various viewpoints are carefully dissected and presented more to the policy and decision makers, who in their diversity and level of action, extend from the male or female family head, the rural community or village head, across to the traditional chiefs, government administrative officials, judicial authorities, and up to the Ministers in government.

It is with their ardent hope that each theme and each contributor has initiated and provided at least, an element from which to start and be engaged in reformatting this issue of land tenure, and especially women's land rights and access to land. This is the Cameroonian challenge of the century, and all stake holders are invited to come on board so that with a broadened women's power base, through the consolidation of their land rights, the leakage points through which energies in natural resource management, socio-economic development etc., would now be sealed. The resulting new product (reformed land tenure system), would emerge as one in which the rural Cameroonian woman, in full legality, can undertake all her productive and reproductive actions just as her male counterpart, unperturbed.

The Rural Woman in Cameroon

The Cameroonian rural woman who is being referred to in this discussion is that woman whose abode is in the hinterland of the country, far from much direct urban interferences. She dwells in that abode with her family, of which she may be the family head, her husband, the children and other relatives. The single house or group of houses and barns, which provide the central unit for all her operations, is seated on a piece of family land. From that central unit, she departs, early in the morning to go out and attend to the livestock and crops or to do some hunting, water collection, fuel wood collection or fishing that provides subsistence to the family. It is around this well-structured unit that she has carefully identified the spring or any other water point, and the patch of woodland from which the other necessities of the family are satisfied. Day in and day out, this rural woman determines, through a series of in-built systems, what has to be produced on any part of this land: first for the sustenance of her family and then the excess for the market. This is done either in collaboration with her husband or with the rest of the work force under her roof. She operates in a system that auto-regulates itself without exaggerated external influences. Some of the distinguishing elements in such rural operational units are the woman's contribution to the economic, environmental, and general sustainable management of that unit (the farm), and the ripple effects from each of these land use activities that eventually provide other departure points for operators outside this rural unit. There are over 60% of such rural women in Cameroon with all the potentials earlier cited remaining unharnessed due to gender differences. These gender differences finally play into the common productive assets, with land being central in the present context.

Women and Land in Agricultural Improvement and Socio-Economic Stability

At the Cameroonian national level, the 1987 population and housing census revealed that 51% of the population was female as against 49% male. In the November 2005 population census results, women make up 50.6% of the population as against 49.4% for men. As to the rural/urban population distribution, 51.3% of these women live in rural areas. This high percentage of women residing in rural areas is further confirmed when one examines the situation at a regional level. The situation in the North West region shows that 52.8% of the population is rural as against 47.2% males living in urban areas. There is thus a male deficiency in rural areas which when put within the framework of male migration into big cities and areas of agro-industrial complexes, which finally leaves the identification, harnessing and development of agricultural potentials in the hands of the women. The diversification of Cameroon's agriculture, exhibited either in the ecological zones or in its rain-fed, irrigated, small scale, urban or peri-urban formats remains consequently for the most part the main undertaking of the women.

In their roles as farmers of rain-fed agriculture, carried out on either fragmented small parcels of rented, begged or family land, women plant, weed, and harvest food crops for the family and for the market. When the seasons and climate change or turn negatively against them, they resort to irrigated agriculture for which the use of traditional knowledge systems (for the most part, the identification of topography and types of crops) once more renders their tasks very difficult. The stream and river plains of the North West Region, the Lake Chad, Bamendjin plains and basins stand out as testimonies to these energetic undertakings of the women. It is also worth noting that in times of economic crises, especially during the 1980s in Cameroon, women in urban areas searched and used mostly tiny, unoccupied lands in the urban and peri-urban areas for vegetable, fruit and other food crop production. In the agro-industrial zones of plantation agriculture, they were the first to take up the food

4

production challenge and undertake food crop production with their male counterparts on the small, isolated, infertile parcels of land commonly known as 'chop farms.'

Despite these additional inputs and self-initiated responsibilities in the agricultural realm, Cameroonian women in general have less access to the accompanying resources and services that should increase productivity, earn more income for them, raise the socio-cultural and political status of such women, and ease their burdens in the multiple roles they play in household and caretaking duties. A United Nations agency (IFAD) revealed in September 2010 that food production by women on land over which they have consolidated rights in most countries of Sub-Saharan Africa, Cameroon included, could increase by 10 to 20%.

In the spring of 2001 issue of *Development Outreach*, published by the World Bank, Alan Gelb states that most rural women in Africa have less access to productive assets including land, as well as to such complimentary factors of production as credit, fertilizer, and education. He adds that women are thus likely to have full control over the product of their labor, reducing in consequence inherent incentives to pursue productive income-earning opportunities and/or recurrent reinvestments on such lands. There are thus missed potentials when women are sidelined in matters of equity in land ownership and use. The logical projections according to this World Bank report (Alan Gelb) are: if women enjoyed the same overall degree of capital investment in agricultural inputs, including land, as their male counterparts, output could increase by up to 15%. Also, in shifting or exchanging existing resources that are found on men's and women's arable pieces of land within the same household could increase output by 10 to 20%. So, investing in women through guaranteeing their absolute rights over land in Cameroon remains a fundamental gateway to reducing rural poverty, hunger, unemployment and the cohort of land conflicts and other negative elements that destabilize the communities in rural Cameroon.

Women and Land in Natural Resource and Holistic Environmental Management

Held in Yaounde between the 26th and the 28th of June 2006, the National Assembly of Cameroon in its Regional Seminar for the parliaments of the African states took a positive step in the right direction by treating the issue of capacity building of parliaments on sustainable development. At this meeting, they discussed water and desertification as case studies that could go a long way in addressing and re-addressing issues of environmental management. Among many environmental problems identified with the solutions envisaged were the following:

Table 1: Problems and solutions identified by the Cameroonian law makers

Identified Environmental issue	Solutions envisaged
Environmental protection policies and laws that are not very popular and are difficult to implement because they often take away people's livelihoods by seeking to ease pressure exerted on natural resources (ban on forest exploitation, hunting, fishing, etc.)	Provide affected communities and individuals (males and females) with alternative livelihoods that should go hand in hand with financial, and other productive incentives, including land that is equitably distributed between men and women.
Managing environmental problems often transcends borders and gender.	• Develop a common vision for the sustainable management of the environment that is also inclusive of women and men through awareness raising and capacity building. • Involve more women in finding solutions and implementing them at such local levels.

From the problems and solutions identified in Table 1 by the Cameroonian law makers, one notices a gradual, but significant step being taken to uplift and uphold existing measures and the mechanisms that the women are single-handedly putting in place. The Cameroonian woman with her knowledge of preparing, smoking, and drying fish when it is brought home by her male counterpart can then fully participate in any positive environmental improvement and corrective alternatives on which she has adequate information. She can develop her own inland fish ponds to counter the issue of overfishing in the rivers, lakes, and coastal waters. She would be able to undertake selective fuel wood harvesting with which to smoke and dry such fish, only if the family or community land and such necessary investments were equitably distributed between the men and the women. She would quickly understand any issues related to tree planting because she is often faced with the difficulty of collecting wood for cooking or for drying farm produce.

If the law makers went ahead and forcefully implemented the issue of a common vision for the sustainable management of the environment that transcends gender, that of capacity building through seminars and education, then the rural woman would be empowered and provided with adequate knowledge systems and other tools and means with which to operate in each ecological/environmental niche found on the land over which she has customary, traditional and administrative rights. In any case, they (the women) constitute 78 to 80% of the workforce in rural Cameroon, and are often better placed to comprehend most components of the natural resources, which in the global and greater numbers, are located on the land.

Women and Water-related Issues

There is an adage which states that he who wears the shoe knows exactly where it hurts, and so women who, among their multiple household chores cover long distances by day or night to fetch water, know exactly how to efficiently manage that water. They use water for household washing, for watering flocks of animals and also for various types of irrigation. They have, through their daily/seasonal soil management processes and knowledge systems, been able to determine where a water table in a valley or hill slope can be reached with relative ease. It is through this type of performance that the rural women have been able to guess the quality and quantities of water likely to be available for their crops. As a result, they negotiate with landlords to determine rents to be paid in cases where the land is begged or rented for any agro-pastoral activity. If in all these processes the rural woman in Cameroon craves to invest her energy and know-how so as to cultivate such a piece of land, over which she has no water rights, then, what would be the positive long term investments for higher output be if she had recognized rights over that land?

In Yaoundé, Douala, and a few other towns in Cameroon, where well-to-do women have purchased land, registered it, and now have full ownership rights over it, the portions of that land near a slope have often been reserved for home gardens or what is normally known as 'backyard gardens.' On such spots, they carefully exploit the surface soil moisture during the dry season for vegetables, flowers, and other short cycle crop production. In all, the simple fact that their land has a certificate empowers them to undertake long-term plans on urban agriculture.

In Santa area, as well as in the valleys of the few streams that flow across Bamenda town, in the vast plains of Ndop, Dschang, the river Benoue plains of North Cameroon, and many more areas, the multitudes of dry season crop cultivators are women. They are able to determine where to sink bore holes for the much needed water, which, when exploited in sufficient quantities, is used as a social link between those who have it upstream and those who have similar activities downstream. Social relations thus emerge between these groups of farmers, having been established because the woman finds and shares the quantity of water available. The notion of cooperatives, be this production, consumer or export co-operatives has and can take root from such a simple element of bringing people together and working with them, provided in this case that land rights are guaranteed. Water would then be the social link, just as coffee or cocoa is the link in the crop sector.

Cameroonian Rural Women and Forest Resource Exploitation

In Cameroon, the forest is one of the resource bases from which are harvested a variety of products. These products include spices from tree barks, fruits, leaves and roots. The Cameroonian cuisine has, with the use of these products (known as non-timber products), attracted most people to go for Cameroonian dishes whenever and wherever the occasion arises. The same holds true for the medicinal values provided for by these same forest products.

Across various ecological zones of Cameroon, any patches of woodland along difficult mountain slopes and in the river or stream valleys are thus coveted by both men and women. Whoever has tenure rights on the land where such forests, woodlands or their relics are located, claims and determines outright any modalities for their exploitation. It is at this point that issues of concern, especially those gender equity issues, begin to arise and therefore influence the general sustainable management of forest niches and their resources.

Women, for the most part, know how to combine and use the various spices from different parts of a tree or from many trees to improve the quality of the meals they serve day in and day out to their families. They know when and how to harvest, preserve, and even commercialize these products for the welfare of the enlarged family. They have learnt over the years how to preserve some of the plant seeds, their cuttings or roots for replanting, or regeneration of given species. In nearly every village or family circle, some women are highly respected for providing local healing systems, and whose curative elements are derived from forest products. Yet, through unequal or total refusal of land rights, there is unhealthy competition between the men and women in undertaking long-term investments in the sustainable management of such woodlands. There exists, hence, a degradation in both the resource qualities and quantities. Around a coffee, cocoa, plantain or palm oil farm (men's tree crops), a women can only introduce other crops or shrubs, for example the *TephrosiaVegolis* or the *Croton* shrub, (respectively used for fuel wood and attracting honey bees), if the husband accepts. Yet, the *Tephrosia* stems when brought home by the woman are used as fuel wood for heating the home, for drying farm products, and for cooking family meals. The leaves and roots improve on the soil fertility at the farm level. The *Croton* trees provide flowers for high value nectar that bees use for honey production. Whenever the honey is harvested, it serves the family in various ways with financial, medicinal, and nutritional values.

If the woman in this case is unable to exercise and possibly exert her full capacities to plan and follow up each aspect of identifying and making a full inventory of the forest resources on a piece of land over which she has consolidated rights, then the sustainable renewal and even the committed enrichment and protection of these forest resources can only be ephemeral. This has been demonstrated in the case of the Kilum-Ijim community forest management. By incorporating the women in the community management model of Kilum, and by exploring and blending these women's multiple acquired knowledge systems, healthier results of sustainability in an area of patrilineal dominance were attained within shorter periods. If partnership performances of such nature yield such positive results, then the possibility of obtaining higher and more diversified results can be expected whenever women's land rights are assured. The domestication of selected tree or shrub species according to their value succeeds more in this case when the female owner of the land gradually introduces them alongside food crops and/or grazing lots as long-term experimental grounds.

These are the types of long-term plans that have been carried out by the Fulani women and other women groups on plots at Nta-Aya, Mfornta in Bafut Subdivision and some spots along the grazing lands in Jakiri and Sabga in North West Cameroon. Although these plots do not belong outright to the women, the annual in-situ identification, transfer and enrichment of these plots with fodder and medicinal plants has opened up the domains of ethno-veterinary medicine and local pharmacopoeia to these cattle rearing populations. The development of herbarium, backyard medicinal gardens, as well as the construction and yearly maintenance of fodder tree vegetation that serve as live fences to limit the uncontrolled movement of cattle has also emerged in the landscape. All these add value to any piece of land, should it be used as collateral security for loans or other long-term commercial investments.

Rural Women Functionality within the Cameroonian Process of Decentralization

In matters of decentralization, a domain in which Cameroon is advancing, the women, through their proper land rights and empowerment, have much to offer. Once the production base, which is the land, is consolidated, then there will be diversification of investment tools and techniques that arise from a crop, livestock, inland fishing, agro-forestry-pasture base. Confident and assured that such a base is well seated and secured on their own piece of land, the rural women are capable of introducing, adapting, adopting and taking alternatives in their investment ventures, since the crop, livestock, agro-forestry-pastoral and most of the inland fishing activities fall within the framework of their well-mastered daily chores.

The simple end product of all this would be holistic development, consolidation of the women's status, either from the family farm level or the village level, were these agro-pastoral fishing undertakings started. From such activities, and with a blend of local knowledge inputs, natural resources and environmental management dynamics

11

would flow across into financial, economic, administrative and political spheres of the village, council or subdivision, in which the women reside.

In Figure 1: (Spheres of decentralization applied to rural women domains), RD signifies Rural Development. Decentralization departs from single female household heads, male farm groups and mixed female and male groups.

Performing through all or most of these domains and farm groups, which are enunciated on the land to bring about fiscal, economic, political and administrative dimensions, the women become more and more specialized and marketing-oriented. The whole process then as presented in Figure 1 empowers the women to become innovation conveyor agents, whose performances are continuously being improved upon and rendered operational in the context of decentralization and the marketing environment.

An alternative approach to appraising the Cameroonian woman's functionality in her rural environment is that of the sole trader, placed within a well circumscribed environment. This is summarized in Figure 2. In this sole trader marketing environment, there is the initial farm unit (A), also known as the internal environment. At this stage, Cameroonian rural women are well settled on their land. Confidently, either as individual family heads or as groups, and with their self-generated revenue (money) from crop sales, using man power, made up of family members or hired labor, they make decisions on land use systems. Moreover, with their basic machinery (e.g. work tools) etc., they are able to make quick decisions, choices and take alternatives without much male and other external gendered disaggregation interferences playing in.

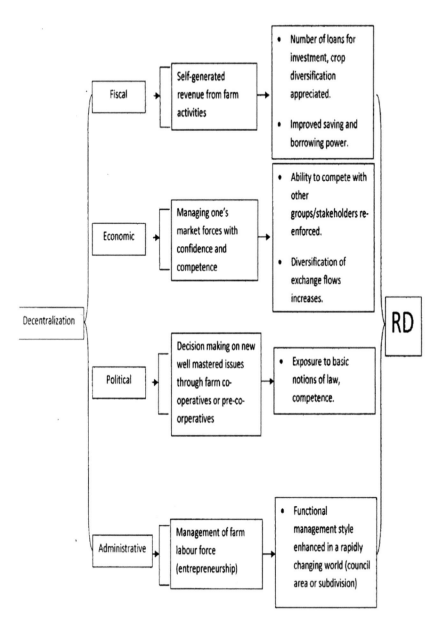

Figure 2: Spheres of decentralization applied to rural women domains. Source: adapted from Ngwa Nebasina (2010)

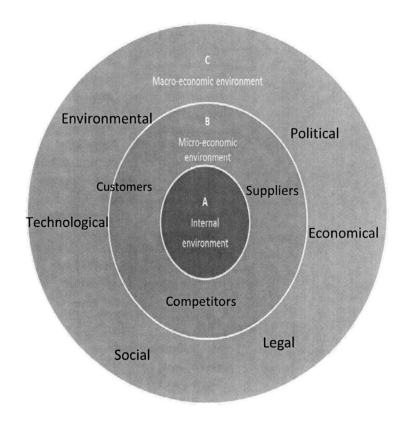

Figure 3: Sole trader's perception of the marketing environment. (Source: Adapted from Blythe (2008)

A) **Internal environment**
- Manpower: Employees' qualifications, training, availability
- Money: Financial status, borrowing power
- Machinery: Types of machines used at farm level
- Methods: Warehousing decisions (buffer stocks)

B) **Micro-economic environment**
- Customers: Farm gate, single and groups.
- Suppliers: Inputs, can be regular or seasonal

C) **Macro-economic environment**
- Political: Legislation, land registration.

- Economical: Market pricing, supply and demand pressures
- Social: People's lifestyle and changing tastes, internal social stability
- Technological: Progress from traditional tools to modern machinery, adoption of improved varieties and species.
- Environmental: Biodiversity, natural and sustainable resource management e.g. response to droughts and floods.
- Legal: Village laws and customs

At the macro-economic environment level (B), the operational notion of sole trader fades gradually. Other rural actors join in, either as customers or suppliers or contributors with innovative ideas or materials. The activities of such actors, consisting of customers and suppliers of farm inputs are now felt at the larger village level, council area level, or sub-divisional level. Activities, decisions, and alternatives taken on the use of land at each of these levels indicated earlier would consequently have added values to such a broadened base.

Simply put, the women's activities at the internal environment as well as at the micro-economic environment level would be greatly enhanced if their educational status, capacity and confidence-building were properly attended to. It is such confidence and educational status that now expose these women to some understandings of the global village exigencies. These exigencies, in essence, revolve around ✳ technological, environmental, population and /or natural resource issues. Therefore, at any operational level, the personally acquired revenue from sales of farm produce, or the skills acquired in managing her farm labor force, the rural woman is fully represented. She has a voice as well as ideas for consideration and implementation.

Moreover, these are the hidden unharnessed potentials which bring about the success stories of the "Buyam sellam" groups of women who operate within the Cameroonian foodstuff distribution channel. A fair percentage of the "Buyam sellam" women have gained the experience of bargaining, rallying other women, and sharing the same business acumen. This has lead women to

15

eventually manage local farm-level cooperative finances and to become empowered to undertake similar functions at higher levels in the society. Empowerments of this nature reveal that the rural woman in Cameroon has much to offer in the decentralization process, whose objectives range from rural development, to environmental management and across to natural resource exploitation for poverty alleviation.

Conclusion

Women's rights and access to land in Cameroon have long been stifled by tradition and blurred judicial and administrative procedures. With the advent of globalization and with the liberalization of the market economy, many possibilities now exist for investments on land. Land ownership rights for women that would enable them to catch up and fit into these current processes of liberalization cannot be allowed to pass by. Also, this is an era when world issues are being brought down from a generalized global level to door step, village, and farm-gate levels for efficient and profitable implementation.

Rural Cameroon has much to offer to the outside world through its management of genetic resources, bio-diversity, and huge rural forest potentials for carbon sinks. By diversifying and consolidating the departure base, which is provided by women's rights and access to land, the Cameroonian rural woman would be empowered to develop entrepreneurial attributes.

As Cameroonian family heads, community chiefs or leaders, government administrative and judicial officials read through the viewpoints and proposals of the various contributors in this publication, let us all bear in mind that we must be counted as pioneer forerunners who supported the advocacy of women's land rights in Cameroon. Changes of this nature would greatly impact the agro-pastoral, environment, socio-economic and political status of the Cameroonian woman, of the local economy, and of the entire Cameroonian population at large.

References

Agarwal B. (1994), Land Rights for Women, Making the Case, in *A Field of One's Own, Gender and Land Rights in South Asia, Cambridge University Press.*

Gelb A. (2001), Gender and Growth in *Development Outreach.* A special report of the World Bank, Vol. 3, No. 2, Washington D.C

Blythe J. (2008), Essentials of Marketing, Fourth Edition

Ekins P. (1992), A New World Order: grassroots movements for Global change New York, Routledege.

IFAD (2010), Women and Rural Development, Rome, IFAD

Mope P., Bitondo D. (2010), Gender and the assessment of the impacts of land violence in Ndop Plain, North West Region of
✱ Cameroon in *Regard multidisciplinaires sur les conflits fonciers et leurs impacts socio-economico-politiques au Cameroun* Laboratoire de Developpement durable et Dynamique territorial, Universite de Montreal, Pages 223-234

Ngwa N.E., (2010), Understanding Geographic Thought and Concepts in Geography (updated edition) University of Yaounde I

Ngwa N. E. and Mbih R.,(2010), Settlement, Grazing or Agricultural Land: A Platform for Integration or Conflicts in Mezam Division (North West Cameroon) Laboratoire de Developpement durable et Dynamique territorial, Universite de Montreal, Pages 203-212

Ngwa N E., (2000), Local Community Efforts Towards Sustainable Management of Baseline Natural Resources in NW and W Cameroon in *Cameroon Geographical Review,* Vol. 2, Pages 133-153

Chapter Two

Equal Rights but Unequal Power over Land: Rethinking the Process of Engendering Land Ownership and Management in Cameroon

Lotsmart N. Fonjong

Abstract

This paper gives an overview of the issues of gender, power and women's land rights with focus on Cameroon. It highlights the state of women's land rights in which women have mere access but not control; in spite of the fact that they make up a majority of agricultural work force and more than 50% of the world's population. The paper further lays emphasis on how women's right to land depends on their relationship with men: either as husbands, fathers, brothers or male relatives.

It notes that gender dynamics and women's land rights reveal gender discrimination and unequal access and ownership to land. Unequal access and ownership result from land tenure systems which are mostly culture specific and gender power relations which are rooted in patriarchy. The argument is that equality laws are not enough without examining the concept of unequal power. This is because customary practices take the place of the tenure law and in most cases override statutory laws which recommend equality of all citizens to land access and ownership. The paper suggests reasons why gender discriminatory customary laws against women's land rights continue to prevail over statutory rights. It concludes with possible actions for land reforms in Cameroon and advances the basis on which land reforms in Cameroon can be engendered.

Introduction

Cameroon comprises of diverse ethnic groups who are governed by both the statutory and the customary laws. The degree of people's attachment to either of these laws depends on whether they live in urban or rural areas. Customary rather than the statutory law is the actual living law in most of rural Cameroon. Usually most customary laws are designed by men to serve their interests and so doing contradicts the statutory laws in the course of implementation and affects women generally as a group. Generally, women are increasingly facing insecure access to land and limited tenure rights[1]. In addition to women, many if not most pastoralists, smallholders, and occupants of informal settlements in urban and peri-urban areas lack secure rights to land. This insecurity thus constrains their ability to invest, produce and contribute to family livelihood and community development.

Nonetheless, evidence in some areas of Cameroon suggests some progress is being made in increasing women's rights to land and tenure security. In urban and peri-urban areas some women have taken advantage of opportunities offered by statutory laws to purchase or rent plots, while in some rural areas, women farmers are developing multiple avenues (e.g., church membership, common initiative groups and cooperatives) through which to access land and become less dependent on their husbands for land and other derivatives of land. These changing trends can be attributed to: the difficulties of maintaining discriminatory customary practices in a fast evolving world where most of the customary arguments no longer hold; the fact that private ownership of land and property is fast

---

[1] There two basic rights to land: access and ownership rights. Access rights have to do with limited rights without total control over the land or the power to dispose of the land. In this case, there is no security of tenure. Ownership rights (both under customary or statutory laws) have to do with control and decision making over the land and security of tenure acquired through inheritance and land registration. In most cases, women have only access otherwise known as user' rights to land.

20

replacing communal land; and finally the increase in the number of female-headed households.

Cameroon is on the verge of a new family code, which is expected to govern issues of marital property rights. This law potentially could be another step in helping women to realize their constitutional promise of equality. Efforts like public awareness campaigns and support for women's legal aid would help women and men learn about the requirements of the law and give them practical knowledge about how land rights can legally be transferred within families and between generations. Any law or legal reform in the domain of property rights in Cameroon today must reflect the complexities and realities of its present society where individual survival no longer depend on the invisible man and head of household.

Based on a review of the concept of power and rights, this paper examines the context of gender inequality in land rights in Cameroon. It discusses land reform options and recommendations that can ensure equal rights and equal power for men and women in land ownership and management in the country. The paper makes use of primary and secondary data and is based on imagery constructed from both sources. The primary sources included field observations and survey which was part of a wider study across the country. Theories of power and rights provided the theoretical framework underlying the analysis in this paper. Furthermore, examples from studies where land reforms have been attempted provided valuable lessons that can be useful for the situation in Cameroon.

Contextualizing Issues of Rights and Women's Empowerment

Proponents of the rights-based approach argue that women's rights can be seen as elements in the "social base of self-respect." Sen (2000) holds that millions of people living in developing countries are not free. He argues that even if they are not slaves in the sense of the term, they are denied elementary freedom and remain imprisoned in one way or another by economic poverty, social deprivation, political tyranny or cultural authoritarianism. Based on human rights approach, a onetime Nobel Prize winner, Mutangadura believes that the rights to use and control land are central to the lives of rural women in countries where these natural resources are major sources of income and livelihoods. From these perspectives, the quest for women's land ownership goes beyond the acquisition of land rights just for rights' sake. The lack of land inheritance and other ownership rights by women indicates they are victims of discrimination since land is considered a fundamental resource to women's living conditions, economic prosperity, social cohesion, and political empowerment. Without rights to land, women's socio-economic and political agenda including physical security is compromised.

Women's land tenure rights determine not only their household level of living and livelihood, but also food security (ILO, 1996). Rights-based approach advocates argue that more gender-equal land rights for women can enhance productivity. Secure land rights for women increase their output by improving women's access to credit. There is need for countries and international communities to protect the land rights of women since these rights are crucial for their sustained livelihood and empowerment. Without the recognition of these rights by society, women remain mere tenants even on land that has never before been owned by any individual or community. For instance, there are cases where women have independently opened up new farm lands in thick and inaccessible bushes and forests in Cameroon only for the men (who, unaided, cannot locate the actual boundaries of such lands) to later on claim ownership when these lands become productive and accessible.

Women's empowerment according to the United Nations Guidelines on Women's Empowerment, 'has five components: women's sense of self-worth; their right to have and to determine choices; their right to have access to opportunities and resources; their right to have the power to control their own lives, both within and outside the home; and their ability to influence the direction of social change to create a more just social and economic order, nationally and internationally. Power is a critical aspect of women's

22

empowerment. Power is used here to reflect its traditional notion in the social sciences as the ability to exercise influence and control (Lips, 1991) over others regardless of their own wishes and interest ? (Weber, 1946). Weber sees power as the probability that an actor within a social relationship would be in a position to carry out his will despite resistance to it. He thus links power with the concepts of authority and rule with the ultimate goal of domination for economic and other interests. Although Weber is interested in power as a factor of domination based on economic or authoritarian interests, men's perceptions of power over land go beyond economic interest alone to include socio-political dominance over women. This is because power is a relational phenomenon and according to Polsby (1970, 3), should be analyzed on the basis of "…who participates, who gains and who loses from alternative outcomes, and also who prevails in decision making." Power thus, does not exist for power's sake but can be instrumental in acquiring, exercising and protecting legitimate rights which could otherwise be violated. This sometimes involves conflict. Page and Czuba (1999) argue in this light that since power is created in a relationship; both power and relation can change and they see empowerment as that process of such change. Kabeer (2011) believes that empowerment is the ability of women to make strategic choices. It therefore involves gaining strategic space which was hitherto deprived in an individual or a group.

Although equal rights over land and other resources might, in principle, exist, it does not necessarily translate into equal power since rights and power are not the same. Thus, while statutes in Cameroon might actually advocate for gender equality of land rights, men, by virtue of their power base, control the land and render the women landless because they are powerless. This situation leads men to directly or indirectly dictate the activities of women on the land, making women's empowerment and rights to become two sides of the same struggle. Women need to exercise power so as to be able to claim and protect their land rights.

Equality in land rights is a critical element in women's economic empowerment but, women most often have only use rights; they cannot own land which is a source of livelihood for family. Endowing women with land will empower them economically as well as strengthen their ability to challenge social and political gender inequalities. But one must be careful not to rush to premature conclusions on women actually achieving empowerment without a careful review of the type of empowerment. This is because it is easier for women in developing countries to be able to attain some level of collective empowerment particularly in the public while being stripped of any form of empowerment within the household because of fear and ignorance. Thus, the public and the private are different and as Kabeer observes, successes in the public domain is hardly seen in the domestic sphere. Legislations and land reforms alone cannot bring about true successes in women's rights and empowerment in both the public and domestic spheres without fundamental changes in men's power and gender power relations both at home and in the public.

Rethinking of Women' Land Rights

Women comprise more than half of the world's population but rarely do they own any reasonable forms of property, neither do they have adequate access to land nor make major decisions pertaining to the allocation and usage of such property. In Africa, agriculture constitutes the core of most economies with women contributing over 80% of the workforce (Boserup, 1970). However, this contribution is often obscure in national production statistics because: 1) most of it takes place in the informal sector and 2) of the fact that women are mostly seen as wives rather than partners with men in development. As a result, women at best have users' rights, which are in turn dependent on the nature of their relationship with men either as husbands, fathers, brothers or male relatives. In some communities like the Beti of Southern Cameroon, women may obtain access to land through a male relative. Nonetheless, this access may also entail limitations on the uses of the land (Guyer, 1984, Fonjong et al 2011). Women cannot inherit the land but are granted food plots

24

by their husbands on which they cannot plant cash crops[2] ~~perennial~~
(Koopman, 1983). It therefore follows that women's access to land can be denied at any time, as it is dependent on the whims of male benefactors.

Women's limited access to land and security of property rights have emerged as critical constraints on increasing agricultural productivity. For example, they are unable to invest and take major decisions on land because they do not own it. Notwithstanding, the situation of women in relation to land is not homogenous across the board, as there are some women who do not have problems with land ownership. Elite women can buy and own land like men but the number of such women particularly in rural Cameroon is insignificant when compared to their landless counterparts who do not have the means and power to do so. And so, rights and power as applied over land is not only limited to gender but is also limited to class and thus require a multidimensional analysis in understanding their dynamics.

Gender dynamics and use of land

While the category 'women' is not a homogenous[3] one, men and women (even as husband and wife) can be very different with different interests. Men and women perform different gender roles[4] which are socially/culturally determined and thereby differ across different societies. Differences in gender roles results in men and women having different interests and uses over land. Kumar 1987; Randolf 1988; Koopman 1993, explain the distinction between traditional cash crops and export crops which are "male crops," while

---

[2] Cash crops are most often perennial, a longer gap between planting and initial harvest as opposed to food crops. So insecurity is greater when is used for food crops as opposed to cash crops

[3] Women as a category are different in terms of class, age, marital status, co-wives, etc. with different privileges, power and opportunities.

[4] Women are generally considered home managers who should be preoccupied with immediate services such as food and care provision while men are expected to be involve long term projects that will generate income to take care of costly projects like construction, funeral, etc.

25

subsistence crops are "female crops." Women use land to grow crops for immediate family consumption while men are responsible for providing cash income and so are said to grow cash and export crops. As seen earlier, the power over land in most Cameroonian societies rests with the head of the household. More men than women are heads of households and land is mainly controlled by male households on the assumption that land is held in trust for all in the households. In Kenya, just like in Cameroon, Kameri-Mbote (2005) observes that men household heads control land because community authorities who are predominantly male have allocated the land to male household heads and these lands are passed down to male heirs, making access to land for most females dependant on their relation to these male heirs.

Women and men have different interests in land[5]; moreover, they exercise different authority and power over resources. Customary law tends to be defined by men and are not codified. It gives men customary inheritance rights while women are assumed to be transient within the polity and therefore not strategic as grantees of rights to land, which constitutes the core of a community's existence (ibid). Even more, women and men have different life opportunities. Worthy of note is the fact that the law, policy makers and administrators in the land tenure and management of lands often neglect these important differences, which eventually shape the lives of men and women. The results of all of these are gender discrimination and unequal access to land which may sometimes be unintentional.

defn A land tenure system refers to the terms and conditions under which rights to land are acquired, retained, used, disposed of or transmitted. Tenure systems vary from one community to another and are influenced by the unique historical development of each political grouping and consequent variation of legal and institutional structures. These tenure systems are culture specific and dynamic--

---

[5] Men have more economic and political interest over land than women whose interests are dominantly social.

changing as the social, economic and political situations of groups change. In the case of Africa, this dynamism is seen in how colonization has affected African tenure system by introducing both the notions of state control and private ownership of land.

Whatever the case, a land tenure system is dictated by three factors: people, time and space. Kameri-Mbote (2005) believes that insofar as people are concerned, it is the interaction between different persons that determines the exact limits of the rights any person has over a given parcel of land. These rights are not absolute since there are rules that govern the manner in which the person with tenure is to utilize their rights. Next, there is the Time- Legal framework. Time aspects of tenure determine the duration of one's rights to land, that is how long tenure does last under an existing tenure arrangement. Finally, is the Space-legal pluralism, which embodies the state, custom and religion of the people. The spatial dimension of tenure may be difficult to delineate in exclusive terms since different persons may exercise different rights over the same space at different times.

An outcome of land tenure systems is gender disparity in land ownership across the world, resulting in a situation whereby women constitute less than 20% of land holders. In Central and West Africa, women own less than 10% while in Latin America and Southern Africa more than 30% of land is owned by women. This means that comparative to men, women have limited rights to land. According to Walker (2002), some countries still have legislative barriers to married women owning land in their own right because they are regarded as minors or chattels. Generally women's right to land are secondary rights, derived through their membership in households and secure primarily through marriage. Moreover, women's parcels of land are generally smaller and of inferior quality than those owned by their male counterparts. Even more, sometimes these lands are vulnerable to forfeiture or erosion of various kinds. Barnes 1983, Jackson 1985 and Alwang and Siegel 1994 report that women's landholdings may be less fertile and more distant from the homestead. This again suggests that gender equality of rights without revisiting existing power relations at home is only part of the women's story.

Land policies and legislations in some African countries do not prioritise gender equity. In most countries, land redistribution policies undermine women with secondary rights to land. Therefore, women are not targeted as potential beneficiaries but rather they are targeted as members of groups. Even when attempts are made to formalize indigenous land tenure systems (communal to private), such attempts have contradictory effect on women. Haahr, (2004) explains that in Niger under the existing tenure, the customary system has no female inheritance rights; girls are not granted family land. Women are usually confined at home and most often have neither seen nor know where their husband's landed properties are located. The largest family land is managed by the household head (most often a male) while the smaller piece is given to male children at the age of 15. Very often, girls are already married by age 15 and can have access to a small piece of their father's land only at their husband's permission. This piece of land is considered lent (not a gift) and must be returned if the couple divorces. The situation is even worse for co-wives who are not easily granted access to family land. In a nutshell, the current situation of gender discrimination has fundamental effects, which place women in a precarious position and jeopardize their survival and livelihoods and consequently stifle their effective role and contribution to national development.

Why this Gender Discrimination in Land Ownership

Cameroon's formal law includes a mix of progressive and traditional provisions. The 1996 Constitution provides for all persons to have the right to own property and mandates equality of the sexes and principles of non-discrimination. However, Cameroon's laws of succession and marital property allow for patrilineal control of property. Gender power relations are rooted in patriarchy. Patriarchy literally means the rule of fathers, but today, the meaning goes beyond to include the rule of husbands and other male influences in the society. It is thus all about male dominance, where men as a social class have power over women as another class perceived as second class citizen. This under-rating of women is not with regard to land alone. It is not long that women in most developing countries gained the right to vote or receive votes. The power relations that ensued are socially constructed and are based on economic, ideological and political thinking rather than on biological or natural determination.

Culturally, patriarchy in most cases tends to devalue women's work or achievements and go ahead to portray women as natural, biological creatures who are not only inherently different but also inferior vis-à-vis men. This confers authority to adult males as crucial decision makers, controllers of material resources as well as controllers/managers of women and children's productive and reproductive capacities. According to Lehman in Wangari, the marginalisation of women through cultural norms that discriminate against them, as well as a lack of access to secure livelihoods and basic necessities are part of the issues that entrench rural women in poverty. She continues by saying that traditional cultural practices hinder women's development as it gives men negotiating and decision making power while limiting women's ability to accumulate social power and economic assets.

In addition, patriarchy also describes the form of male domination in terms of the household authority of the father. It directly brings forth the depth of women's exploitation and oppression and can be likened to capitalism especially in terms of access to and control over a society's productive resources. In fact, patriarchy denotes the totality of oppressive and exploitative relations between men and women as in the case of current land tenure systems in Cameroon and Africa when viewed through the gender lens.

Customary Laws in Cameroon

Patriarchy is embedded in customs and manifests itself through customary practices. Bennet (1995) holds that people bound by this custom take it for granted as part of their everyday life experiences. Customs in principle, exclude outsiders who only get an account of them, or are told or read about these customs. But Cameroonian villages, towns and cities are becoming more cosmopolitan, posing a serious threat to some of the obnoxious customs. Yet, where these customs are still surviving as in the Cameroon grass fields, they continue to discriminate against women. In the case of land, these customs hold that:

- Succession always follows the male line even within matrilineal societies;
- Women will at the end of the day get married and take away family property to another family;
- Historically, women do not own land;
- They mostly have user rights over land, and finally
- Were formerly considered as men's property.

The Ineffectiveness of Statutory Provisions

While the Land Ordinances, subsequent Decrees and ministerial Orders all do not discriminate against women (gender neutral)[6], they are not gender sensitive. The problem arising from this is the gap between policy and commitment and the fact that gender equality is not a priority for policy objectives. In fact, no serious attention is given to gender sensitive planning beyond isolated projects that do not have far reaching impacts.

---

[6] It is not possible for a gender neutral constitution and laws to be effective in a gender sensitive cultural context where the 'living law' or day to day practices discriminate against women.

Limitations of Legal Enforcement of Women's Land rights in Cameroon

Although the Cameroon constitution and subsequent statutes give men and women equal rights over land, the civil codes and administrative practices sometimes contradict these in the following aspects:

1. It gives husbands the ability to stop wives' activities, in cases where he thinks her activities endanger the wellbeing of the family.

2. There is no clear provision on the land registration form for application for joint land registration. _practised?_

3. The conceptualization of the notion of head of households by many laws/communities still excludes women and where land is handed to heads of households, women are excluded. A consequence of such a conceptualization/perception was seen in Vietnam in 1998 where the government of Vietnam awarded land titles to households who had farmed on land for long. The consequence of considering only heads of households was that 90% of titles were given to men while very few women benefitted from this endeavour. Even though women were those farming the land, it was the men that got the title since few women were considered heads of households.

4. Up until today, many Mayors are still celebrating marriages according to native laws and customs which subsume women under men.

5. There are usually no clear campaigns that target women who are ignorant of legal provisions and protection of their land rights.

As a result of the above mentioned perspectives, women's inability to own land limits their contribution to sustainable livelihood. However, given that about 70% of Cameroonian rural women depend on land for household survival, there is need for engendering customary practices in the process of land reforms in Cameroon. There are strong economic, political and social arguments to sustain this.

The Basis for Engendering Land Reforms in Cameroon

The issue of gender sensitive land reforms in Cameroon is the quest for a policy option rooted in clear socio-economic and political arguments. Land reform for reform's sake is not enough but reforms should be able to contribute to the improvement of the general well-being through poverty reduction and greater participation of the masses in the process of nation building. Economically, it is believed that ensuring women's land rights would enhance agricultural productivity and economic growth. Since women constitute over 70% of the agricultural workforce, they are closely associated with food crop production and distribution that ensure food security, fight hunger and poverty, and provide raw materials for the industrial sector. Without security of land tenure, women cannot risk to invest in land that will improve agricultural yields, since men make the long term decisions over the land. Secondly, because women's agricultural production is largely for household subsistence, engendering land reforms will provide critical support to their multiple livelihood strategies. This would have direct impact on their welfare as well as their households' with far-reaching impact on labour performance in the larger economy.

Politically and socially, equal access and control over land is a fundamental human right and nobody should be discriminated on the basis of their sex. Engendering land reforms is a fight against injustices and recognition of women's human rights. It bridges the power gap between men and women as women are empowered to make strategic decisions and choices on land. When this happens, gender-based conflicts and domestic violence/injustices are checked. As a source of economic power, engendering the process of land ownership will enhance women's political powers, promote their participation in politics and foster the national processes of democracy, representation and the protection of human rights.

Opportunities for Land Reforms

All things considered, one cannot overlook the legal attempt by the government of Cameroon to create some sort of a level ground for both men and women to own land. But this effort is grossly inadequate and ill adapted to realities, thereby producing a situation of persistent inequality since there is no real equality without equal power. These failures can be overturned if the following careful planning and land reforms are carried out:
-   To involve administrative and policy reforms
-   To include gender capacity building to ensure that land managers, law and policy makers are aware and conscious of the importance of gender in the administration and enforcement of land policy and
-   In a manner that facilitates removal of patriarchal social relationship in society.

The success of these elements will depend on government ability to settle on the right type of land regime on which to guide its policy orientation. That is why Table 1 presents possible options with inherent merits and demerits that can be readapted to suit the Cameroon situation. However, it is not sufficient to discard the customary or the current land tenure practices and to be replaced with another form of gender insensitive system that only aggravates the situation of women. It must be well thought out, based on available options as illustrated in Table 1 and the means on hand to drive the reform process through.

Table 1: Possible Option for Equitable Land Reforms in Cameroon

	Common types	Characteristics
1	Land nationalization (very common after independence)	- Land rights are vested in the hands of the state ; - Assert the power of the state over traditional chiefs, and local communities; - Planning is centralized with little opportunities for liberalization.
2	Land registration/ titling	- Leads to private land ownership; - May exacerbate gender discrimination if women did not have equal rights as men in the traditional system.
3	Land redistribution and resettlement	- Ensures that everyone can access land; - But has to guard against wastage and that those who really need land have enough; - May increase food insecurity and poverty.
4	Land affirmation and recognition	- Reorganization of customary land rights - Transformation of users 'rights into permanent and secured rights; - The process must be decentralized to attract participation; - May widen the inequality and poverty gaps if not well implemented.
5	Inducement, market-assisted initiatives	- Privatization of state farms, state grants and credit schemes to acquire land; - May lead to land remaining in the hands of a few if not well planned to avoid corruption and favoritism.

None of the reform options on Table 1 provide a one-stop solution to gender discrimination in land ownership, particularly in the absence of an enabling environment for governance. The choice should be based on the premise that the administration of the law can occasion the subordination of women. It should also take into consideration the fact that the socio-economic realities and patriarchal ideology pervading the society can further prevent the translation of abstract rights to real substantial rights. Women's rights must be clearly defined in any reform process borrowing from the lesson that gender neutral legal rules and principles governing land in many instances result in de facto gender discrimination. This is because there are compelling facts that land policies and administration are sometimes influenced by administrators' values, attitudes and judgement of women's abilities, which have for long tilted towards women's submission and disempowerment. Thus, the reform process should be one that takes care of this and creates avenues for women to be able to participate more directly and effectively in land management structures like the Land Consultative Board.

Conclusions

Development as construed today has among its core values the reduction of inequalities and strengthening human rights. Attaining these core values are some of the 'musts' not mere options to countries like Cameroon, which aspire to become emerging economies in the nearest future. The stakes are even higher when these core values are narrowed down to issues relating to women who are the engine of development and growth. Consequently, just as women are agents of development, they also need development. Not all development is worthwhile and true development is both gender and results driven. Good governance, particularly resource governance, is crucial to attaining true development. Policies and structures that regulate land and other resources must be well thought out so as to avoid deprivation and discrimination that are likely to breed mistrust from the population and generate resource-based conflicts, which only go to stifle development. And so the construction of power which today is gender-driven needs to be reconstructed to reflect the contribution of distributed roles on an individual to the community or society.

This paper has stressed the fact that equality of land rights cannot be possible for women and other vulnerable groups simply by legal provisions or in the absence of mechanisms that provide for equal power relations. Effective democratic and enforcement mechanisms must accompany the act of law and this explains why land distributions, redistribution and registration should not be directed towards heads of households but towards individuals because households are gender differentiated. Gender is an important determinant of social relations and rights in rural communities. It shapes individuals' opportunities, aspirations, standards of living, access to resources, status and self-perception. The gender socialisation process defines men's and women's priorities concerning land development and use differently. However, given that land is such a critical resource for individual and collective empowerment, it is critical that gender is mainstreamed into its policies, ownership and management.

Rural women like their male counterpart needs to exercise their rights over land which according to Katz and Chamorro (2003), Quisumbing and Maluccio (2003) increases women's bargaining power within households and thereby increase household welfare. That is why there is need for a good legal machinery and support structures that meet the gender-specific reality of a people in society. For as long as we live in a society where women and men follow different paths in life and have different living conditions, with different needs and potentials, rules of law will necessarily affect men and women differently (Tove, 1987).

Recommendations for Engendering the Process of Land Reforms in Cameroon

The following are proposals for engendering the process of land reforms in Cameroon.

1. The government of Cameroon should develop an inclusive land policy and land reform process by

a. Considering the gender dimension in the early stages of the reform and not at the end or implementation phase

b. Accompanying enforcement with a broader support to reforms through sensitization of stakeholders. The process should begin with sensitization and mobilization of a larger range of stakeholders (civil society organization, field staff, men, women, interest groups, administrators and not the other way round)

c. Improving the production and availability of sex disaggregated data relating to production; incomes; contributions; ownership; etc.

d. Consciously making provisions for the inclusion of women in land management decision making structures such as: the Land Consultative Boards, Parliamentary committees of inquiries, laws/policies making committees, etc.

2. De-complexing the land laws and land registration process. Effective enforcement mechanism must be put in place to accompany the act of law. Land rights are governed by different texts, ordinances, which are often contradictory and ambiguous; these texts should be codified and simplified. Moreover, customary and statutory land laws need to be harmonized. Land distribution, redistribution and registration should not be directed towards heads of households but towards individuals because household heads are gender differentiated.

3. Improve women's education. Women generally constitute most of the uneducated in society. They lack basic education and knowledge on how social and legal matters function. As a result, they do not possess the financial resources, knowledge and capacity to go against social norms and would be afraid to exercise their legal rights.

4. The state and civil society organizations should devote resources to improve women's knowledge of legal matters through legal literacy programs and training on how to access institutions that protect and enforce their rights.

5. Increase women's representation in administrative (Land Boards, Lands department, civil administration) and elective offices (Village councils, parliament) that deal with land may help to overcome their social and cultural constrains to land by challenging some of the gender discriminatory practices.

6. Sensitization through the media, courts decentralization structures on the importance of women's land rights will help to change local attitudes at both family and community levels which are hostile to women gaining independent rights to land.

7. Affirmative action to counter discrimination: representation, sale of state land, and further decentralisation of land registration to district level for accessibility, one stop shop for land certificate, etc.

References

Alwang, J., and P.B. Siegel. 1994. Rural Poverty in Zambia: An Analysis of Causes and Policy Recommendations. Washington, D.C.: Human Resources Division, Southern Africa Department, the World Bank.

Barnes, G. (1983). "The Role of Land Tenure in Development." South African Survey Journal, 19 (114), pp. 37-42

Bennett, T. W. (1995). *Human Rights and African Customary Law: under the South African Constitution.* Cape Town: Juta.

Boserup, E. (1970). The Role of women in Economic Development. New York, St Martin Press

Doss, C.R. (1999). *Twenty-Five Years of Research on Women Farmers in Africa: Lessons and Implications for Agricultural Research Institutions; with an Annotated Bibliography.* CIMMYT Economics Program Paper No. 99-02. Mexico D.F.: CIMMYT

Fonjong L., Sama-Lang I. and Fombe L. (2010). An Assessment of the Evolution of Land Tenure System in Cameroon and its Effects on Women's Land Rights and Food Security. *Perspectives in Global Development and Technology:* PGDT 9, 154-169

Guyer, J.1. (1984). Family and Farm in Southern Cameroon. Boston, MA: African Studies Centre, Boston University.

Haahr, M. (2004). How Land Scarcity is Eroding Women's Rights: The Case of Female Seclusion. In Reclaiming Rights and Resources (women, poverty and Environment) *care.ca/ sites/ default/ files/ files/ publications/ Reclaimin-Rights07.pdf*

Fonjong, L.et al. (2011). Land tenure Practices and Women's Right to Land: Implications for Access to Natural Resources in Anglophone Cameroon. IDRC Research Brief No. 1

ILO (1996). Women access to land still restricted by tradition. *Women International Network News, 22, 4.*

Jackson. C. (1985).*The Kano river irrigation project.* Women's Roles and Gender Differences in Development Series 4. West Hartford USA: Kumarian Press.

Kabeer, N. (2010). Women's Empowerment, Development Interventions and the Management of Information Flows. IDS Bulletin, 41: 105–113. doi: 10.1111/j.1759-5436.2010.00188.x

Kameri-Mbote, P. (2005). The Land has its Owners! Gender Issues in Land Tenure under Customary Law in Kenya. IELRC. Switzerland

Katz, E. and Juan Sebastian Chamorro. (2003). "Gender, Land Rights, and the Household Economy in Rural Nicaragua and Honduras." Paper presented at the annual Conference of the Latin American and Caribbean Economics Association, Peubla, Mexico, October 9-11

Kumar, S.K. (1987). Women's role and agricultural technology. In J.W. Mellor, C.L. Delgado, and M.J. Blackie (eds.), Accelerating Food Production in Sub- Saharan Africa. Baltimore, Maryland: Johns Hopkins University Press. Pp. 135–47.

Koopman, J. (1993). The Hidden Roots of the African Food Problem: Looking within the Rural Household. In N. Folbre, B. Bergmann, B. Agarwal, and M. Floro (eds.), *Women's Work in the World Economy*. New York: New York University Press. Pp. 82–103.

Lips, H. (1991). Women, men and power. Mountain View, CA: Mayfield.

Mutangadura, G. (2004). Women and Land tenure rights in southern Africa: A Human Rights- based Approach. London: Church House, Westminster

Page, N., & Czuba, C. (1999). Empowerment: What is it? Journal of Extension, 37(5), 24–32.

Polsby, N. (1970). Community Power and Political Theory. Yale, Yale University Press,

Quisumbing, A. (1996). Male-Female Differences in Agricultural Productivity: Methodological Issues and Empirical Evidence. World Development, 24, 10, 1579-95.

Rainbolt , G.W (2006). Rights Theory. Philosophy Compass. 003(1-11) Blackwell

Randolph, S. (1988). Constraints to Agricultural Production in Africa: A survey of Female Farmers in the Ruhengeri Prefecture of Rwanda. *Studies in Comparative International Development* 23: 78–98.

Sen, A. (2000). Development as freedom. Anchor Books.

Tove, S. D. (1987). Women's Law: An Introduction to Feminist Jurisprudence. Norway: Oslo, Norwegian University Press

United Nations. Guidelines on Women's Empowerment http://www.un.org/popin/unfpa/taskforce/guide/iatfwemp.gdl.html (June 23rd 2011)

Walker, C. (2002). "Land Reform in Southern and Eastern Africa: Key Issues for Strengthening Women's Access to and Rights in Land." In FAO Report. Harare, Zimbabwe: FAO Sub-Regional Office.

Wangari, M. Reclaiming Rights and Resources: Women, Poverty and Environment.

http://care.ca/sites/default/files/files/publications/Reclaimin-Rights07.pdf (accessed online on October 26th 1011)

Weber, M. (1947). *The Theory of Social and Economic Organization*, translated by A M Henderson and Talcott Parsons, 1947, The Free Press and the Falcon's Bring Press

Chapter Three

Women's Inheritance Rights in the North West and South West Regions of Cameroon

Vera N. Ngassa

Abstract

This paper presents the different applicable laws and jurisdictions in Cameroon that deal with the question of inheritance and succession. It also makes a distinction between testate and intestate succession. Using examples from case law, we examine the validity of a will, the place of nuncupative wills and the determination of beneficiaries/administrator. In addition, the paper explains how customary law can influence succession/inheritance rights but at the same time cites situations where some judges have refused to apply custom. It thus discusses the effects of letters of administration, revocation of administration, exceptions to revocation and liabilities, and penalties for administration of estates. We conclude that the applicable laws are conflicting and there is an urgent need to discard archaic and obscure laws and to come up with a concrete, uniform and comprehensive law of succession. Above all, a will by a loving and conscientious testator that recognizes the rights of the surviving spouse and children remain the best way of protecting their rights.

Introduction

In a wider sense, the term inheritance refers to whatever one receives upon the death of a relative based on the laws of descent and distribution. In addition, it could be seen as perpetuity in lands to a man and his heirs or the right to succeed to the estate of a person who died intestate_According to Free online dictionary, inheritance also means anything received from the estate of a person who has died, whether by the laws of descent or as a beneficiary of a will or trust. Black's Law Dictionary on the other hand defines succession as the act or right to a legal or official take- over of a predecessor's office, rank or duties. However, succession in the context of this paper refers to the acquisition of rights or property by inheritance under the laws of descent and distribution.

Although both terms are often used interchangeably in common parlance, the difference between them lies in the fact that inheritance deals with acquisition of property from a deceased relative while succession which is multifarious deals with taking over from a predecessor. This paper deals with how property may be legally transmitted to women upon the death of a predecessor. Although succession is multifarious, the paper is limited to a review of testate and intestate succession. Testate succession or testacy is that which results from a written will or testament executed in the form prescribed by law (footnote). Intestate succession or intestacy on the other hand is that which is established in favour of the nearest relations of the deceased where the deceased left no will. If the deceased is not survived by any relatives, the estate goes to the Crown as *bona vacantia*.

It may be observed that one of the most important differences between testacy and intestacy is that while a man in his will may leave his property to whomsoever he pleases, including strangers and even animals, intestate succession is solely predicated on blood relationship or kinship. In the latter situation, the duty to determine the next best friend or person who is best suited to accede to the deceased's property falls on the courts.

Sources of Law and Applicable Laws

Cameroon is a former British and French mandate territory, which for this reason has multi-jurial legal system. Civil law is applied in French speaking Cameroon while Common law applies in English speaking Cameroon. Both these foreign laws operate alongside a strong under-current of customary laws with the latter sometimes acting as a parallel regime to statutory law. The English common law that is applicable in Anglophone Cameroon includes the common law, doctrines of equity and current English statutes of general application, which by virtue of sections 10 and 15 of The Southern Cameroons High Court laws of 1955, have become incorporated into Cameroon's legal system.

Customary law is part of the country's laws pursuant to the provisions of section 27 of the Southern Cameroons High Court Law 1955, providing that the High Courts shall "observe" and "enforce the observance" of customary law insofar as it is not repugnant to natural justice, equity, and good conscience or contrary to the written law. Moslem law applies in Anglophone Cameroon as part of customary law because the Southern Cameroons High Court Law 1955 states that "native law and custom includes Moslem law." In some areas, some of the foreign received laws have been harmonised into national laws, which take precedence over received law. [7]

Courts with jurisdiction to hear probate matters

It is necessary to discuss the jurisdiction of the courts over probate matters because going to the wrong court will invariably earn

---

[7] The applicable laws would therefore include: 1.The Constitution of the Republic. 2.The Civil Status Registration Ordinance (Ordinance 81-02 of 29 June 1981) particularly Section 77 thereof which deals with widows, section 49 as to the validity of marriage and property settlement and the provisions as to recognition and legitimacy. 3. The Matrimonial Causes Act1973; The matrimonial Proceedings and Family Act 1984; and all current laws on Matrimonial and family matters. 4. The Wills Act 1837and the Wills Amendment Act of 1852 and The Judicature Act 192. 5. The Administration of Estates Act 192. 6. The Supreme Court Civil Procedure Rule Cap 211 of the 1948 Laws, Administrator-General Ordinance, Cap.4 of the1948Laws of Nigeria. 7. The Evidence Ordinance Cap.62 of the1958 Laws of the Federation of Nigeria. 8. The Southern Cameroons High Court Laws 1955. 9. The Non Contentious Probate Rules 1954 as amended by the Non Contentious probate Rules 1987 .10. The Contentious probate Rules 1954 as amended.11. Halsbury's Laws of England 12. The White Book (Supreme Court Practice). 13. The Customary Courts Ordinance, cap.142 of the1948 Laws of Nigeria, as amended by the Adaptation of Existing Laws Order.

the wrong outcome.

i) The High Courts

Matters concerning access to a deceased's property are known as "probate matters" and are heard in the Probate Division of the High Courts. The High Courts are competent in succession matters, arising within their jurisdiction if the deceased had property therein.[8]

ii) Customary and Alkali Courts

The jurisdiction of the above courts is limited to Next-of-kin Declarations in intestate succession over the property of persons subject to customary law, especially customary marriages. In the celebrated case of *Manyi Pauline Evakise v. Joseph Evakise Evelle*,[9] the Supreme Court ruled that customary courts have no jurisdiction over probate matters or construction of wills, which are the sole preserve of the High Courts.

Testate Succession (Testacy)

Testacy describes the situation where a person dies leaving a will. A will is a written document made by an owner of property during his lifetime in which that person clearly leaves instructions as to how his/her property should be managed or divided after his or her death. This document may include any other wishes such as a burial place, arrangement of last burial rites and the installation of the heir or next of kin. Generally English law like French law recognizes and enforces the principle of absolute testamentary freedom as evident in the statement by *Sir Hannen J. in Broughton v. Knight* [10] that a person *"may disinherit... his children and leave his property to strangers to gratify his spite or*

---

[8] See Order 48 Rules 1 and 2 of the Supreme Court (Civil Procedure) Cap. 211 of the 1948 Laws of Nigeria; Section 16(b) as amended by article 16(c) of Law No. 89/019 of 29 December 1989 as amended by Law no 2006/015 of 29th December 2006 which gives the High Court's original jurisdiction over succession except those over which the customary courts are competent.

[9] Estate of Kinge Evakise - 1999 Gender law Report Vol 1.

[10] (1873) L.R. 3P & D. 64, 65-66.

to charities to gratify his pride."

The courts will generally give their blessings to the testator's wishes by granting probate provided the conditions for validity and probate are satisfied. However, the law puts certain checks on whimsical and unjust testators. In this regard, a widow or any other beneficiary excluded from a will by a temperamental testator could sue under The Inheritance (Provision for Family and Dependant) Act 1975 for reasonable financial provision.

Besides, an otherwise valid will may be declared unconscionable as was the case in *Mme Veuve Bebe nee Ekambi Elise c/ Bebe Moise dit Ndoumbe*.[11] Here, the Supreme Court quashed the decision of the lower courts which had upheld a will in which the deceased had disinherited Bebe Moise and other children born to his first wife in favour of his second wife with whom he had no children. It was held by the Supreme Court that the will was unconscionable. Similarly it was in *Jesco Manga Williams v. Helen Otia & Chief Ikome*,[12] held by the Limbe Customary Court that a will in which the deceased left the major part of his property to his friend as against his large polygamous family was repugnant to natural justice, equity and good conscience. It has to be observed that an important exception to testamentary freedom is found in the rule of public policy which precludes any person who has feloniously killed another from taking any benefit under the will of the person he has murdered.

Conditions necessary for a valid will

- *Capacity of the testator.*

The will must be made and signed by the testator himself since it is a cardinal principle of English law that a man may not delegate his testamentary power. The following requirements must also be met.

---

[11] Arret No. 46/L of 4th May 1995.
[12] Civil Suit No. LM/16/97 (unreported).

- *Age*

The testator must be at least 21 years of age. By section 7 of the Wills Act 1837 no will made by any person under the age of 21 years shall be valid. However sections 11 and 5(2) of the Will's Act make exceptions for soldiers in actual military service (including marines or sea men) who are 18 years old because they may die in battle.

- *Mental Capacity*

Persons incapable by reason of mental disorder are under the Mental Health Act of 1995 precluded from making a will. A person suffering from mental disorder may during the continuance of such disorder be incapable of making a valid will as was held in *Bank v. Good fellow*.[13]

- *Absence of other physical impairments*

Old age, illness, blindness or illiteracy may affect a person's testamentary capacity.

- *Absence of Fraud or Cohesion*

If challenged, it has to be shown that the person making the will did so "of his or her own free will." The court may refuse to grant probate where actual force was used to compel the testator, or where the testator was induced by fear or fraud to draw the will. Similarly a court may refuse to prove a will or some part thereof obtained by the importunity of an overbearing wife. In *Marianne Bongyilla v. Che Peter*[14] a will was held to be a forgery because at the time of its purported execution in a lawyer's chambers the deceased was bedridden in hospital with the medical records showing that he lacked the necessary mental capacity to make a will. Furthermore, the ill-fated will wrongly described some of the property, excluded property which ought to have been included and included property which had been sold by the testator.

---

[13] (1870) L. R 5QB 549).
[14] (2006) Appeal No. BCA/48/2003 (unreported)

Form and Contents of Wills

Written Form

The Wills Act 1963 provides that wills must be in writing (except for wills of soldiers in actual service, sea men and even nurses and typists serving the military), but no special form of words is necessary. Nuncupative wills, which are prevalent under customary law, are thus not recognized.

Signature and Attestation Clause

By Section 9 of the Act a will shall be signed at the foot or end by the testator or by some other person in his presence. Section 9 further requires that the testator's signature be made and acknowledged in the presence of the testator by two or more witnesses.

There are other requirements as to executors' interpretation of wills and revocation of wills, which have not been discussed in this paper.

Probate of wills

Order 48 rr 4,5,6,7 & 8 Supreme Court Civil Procedure Rule Cap 211 1948 requires that, for a will to take effect it must be proved by producing a copy thereof certified under seal by the court after the death of the testator. It is an offence for an executor to execute a will without probate.

A will is proved in common form or solemn form. A will is proved in common form when the will is brought to court and at least one of the attesting witnesses testifies under oath that the testament exhibited is true, whole and is the last will and testament of the deceased thereto. A will is proved in solemn form when, as a result of an action brought in court, it is pronounced to be a valid testamentary document. The action may be commenced by the executor, a beneficiary or other person interested in the will or by some person opposed to the will e.g. the widow of the deceased entitled to a share of the deceased's estate on intestacy, a legatee or devisee named in the will who has either not received his due or disputes what is due or an executor or legatee or devisee named in some other testamentary instrument (will) whose interests are prejudiced by the present will (see *Birch v. Birch*[15]).

The place of nuncupative wills post-obit gifts and gifts *inter vivos*

Although the Wills Act 1837 and the Administration of Estate's Act 1925 provide that a will be in writing, yet because of the tradition of venerating the dead, the deceased's wishes though not in written form will still be carried out. A nuncupative will is an oral will while a post –obit gift is an oral declaration made by the deceased in his lifetime, leaving property upon his death to certain beneficiaries. A gift *inter vivos* is an outright gift made during the lifetime of the person who madé the gift. If the deceased makes a gift to a person not considered a beneficiary, the wife or children of the deceased cannot, after the deceased's death, appropriate the property. In the *People v. Elangwe James Netonda*[16] the deceased had in his lifetime made a gift *inter vivos* of part of his farm to his sister on the grounds that his sister had helped developed the farm. When following his death his son, the accused, chased her out of the farm, he was convicted of disturbance of quiet enjoyment.

Intestacy (Intestate Succession)

Unlike under French law, English law has an interim period of administration during which the beneficiaries wait to get into their entitlements. Only after administration and distribution can one properly talk of inheritance. Sections 21 (1) of the Non-Contentious Probate Rules of 1954 and 46(1) of the Administration of Estates Act 1925 provide an outline of potential beneficiaries and administrator

---

15 [1902] p. 130
16 CFIK/Ds/59c/08.

in the following order of priority:

a) The surviving spouse,

b) The children of the deceased or the issue of any such child who has died during the lifetime of the deceased,

c) The father or mother of the deceased,

d) Brothers and sisters of the whole blood, or the issue of any deceased brother or sister who has died, brother and sisters of the half blood or their issue, grandparents, uncles and aunts of the whole blood or their issue. The list ends with uncles and aunts of the half blood or their issue.

Under the civil law system, the children are entitled to inherit first, then the parents and brothers and sisters of the deceased, while the widow comes last and has only a right of usufruct. The right of usufruct is the right under article 600 of the *Code Civil* to use and inhabit the matrimonial home. Where there is money from the estate, the widow may have a right to 1/4 of the proceeds from the estate. Even where there are no children, the widow still does not inherit. The inheritance is given to the nearest male relative as was done in the case in *Minja Jean c/Mengo Marceline.*[17]

Although the above statement of the common law position priorities would give the impression that the rules are rather cut and dried, the administration of estates under the common law is influenced by many other considerations. It is thus apposite at this stage to study some of the considerations that influence the grant of administration and women's inheritance rights.

The Surviving Spouse

The general rule is that if the surviving spouse (in this case the widow) applies, all things being equal, she will be granted letters of administration over and above all other applicants for grant. This rule is supported by precedent, the most celebrated of which is the case of

---

[17] Arrêt No. 314 of 6th August 1987.

51

Nanje Joseph Okia v. James Modika and Ors.[18] It was in the Estate of Nchari,[19] further held by Epuli J as he then was that when a marriage is monogamous, the widow assumes exactly the same position as a widow in England. In Estate of Achidi Mofor,[20] the court in reiterating section 21(1) N.C. Prob Rules 1954(in full) held that the trial judge in granting letters to the caveator, who was a half-brother to the deceased, and in further partitioning the estate 'went outside the scope of his mission and misdirected himself.' The Court of Appeal in revoking the probate letters and granting same to the appellant/widow called the respondent step brother 'a complete stranger in the matter.'

Section 77 (2) of the Civil Status Registration Ordinance further recognizes the widow's right to inherit by providing that: *"in the event of the death of the husband, his heirs shall have no right over the widow, nor over her freedom or the share of property belonging to her. She may, provided that she observes the period of widowhood of 180 days from the date of the death of her husband freely remarry without anyone laying claim to whatever compensation or material benefit for dowry or otherwise, received either at the time of engagement, during marriage or after marriage."*

It is thus obvious that the widow's inheritance rights are strong and if she applies for grant of probate letters she would normally be given. Obstacles to the widow's rights often arise from the fact that while the widow is observing the long period of widowhood of six months, she is overtaken to the courts by the male relatives of the deceased.

The nearest relative is usually considered first.

In the Estate of Baba Nya,[21] the Customary and Appeal Courts in application of Muslim law held that the family of the husband of a deceased widow was entitled to her property against claims made by

---

[18] CASWP/22/91 Judgment of 11th March 1992.

[19] 1999 G.L.R. 59.

[20] Alice Siri Mofor v. John Moforance Mofor CASWP/34/92 reported in 199 Gender Law Report V 1.

[21] (1985) Suit No. C.A.S.W.P/CC/16/85 (unreported).

the appellant, a complete stranger claiming to be the "god-son" of the deceased.

The court's discretion when the applicant-for-grant is unsuitable

The courts have wide discretionary powers to pass over the person who would otherwise have been entitled to the grant of administration and appoint as administrator any other person they deem expedient if, "by reason of any special circumstances" this appears to be necessary. Examples of special circumstances which would justify an objection and a possible passing over of the person with prior rights to a grant include unsoundness of mind, minority, the bankruptcy of the estate, bad character or otherwise unfitness to act, the disappearance or absence of the person entitled. This discretion was justified by Mbeng J. in *Nanje Fabian v. Meta Edward*[22] thus:

> *"I think that the pivotal factor for the court to consider in determining who should administer an estate, especially that of an intestate, is who is capable and honest. It is not a matter of relationship and priority as the administrator may not necessarily be a beneficiary to the estate."*

In Estate of Numbissie Albert Fange[23] the court while confirming R 21(1) of NC Probate Rules under which the surviving spouse comes first stated that "if a dispute arises among persons as to which of them should take grant of letters the court in its discretion selects the person who is most likely to administer the estate to the best advantage or interest of the creditors and beneficiaries." Based on the above, the letters previously granted to the appellant first widow were revoked and granted to the Administrator General of Meme.

---

[22] (2005) Suit No. C.A.S.W.P/53/2002 (unreported).
[23] Noumbissie nee Wanji Mary v. Ngangui John (2002) 1 CCLR p1.

In *Njonji Godlove v. Esther Njonji,*[24] the plaintiff was the son of the deceased from a previous customary marriage while the defendant was the widow of the deceased by a subsequent marriage. Upon the death intestate of the deceased, the family council made the widow successor to her husband. She obtained a next-of-kin declaration and was granted letters of administration. The plaintiff claimed that the letters should be revoked and granted to him because of the improper administration of the estate by the widow and the fact that he was the first child of the deceased. The court, in spite of this contention, appointed the brother of the deceased as the administrator of the estate in the exercise of its discretion.

Appointment of neutral persons in case of stalemate

Where there is animosity between one or more persons contending for grant, the courts could appoint a completely neutral person .This is done pursuant to Order 48 Rule 37 of the Supreme Court (Civil Procedure) Rules of the 1948 Laws of Nigeria which provides that:

> *"In a case of intestacy, where the peculiar circumstances of the case appear to the court so to require, the court may, if it thinks fit, on the application of any person having interest in the estate of the deceased, or of its own motion, grant letters of administration to an officer of the court or to a person in the service of the Government."*

In Estate of Noumbissie, [25]a cousin to whom letters were later granted after the grant to the first widow was revoked, connived with one of the widows to mismanage the estate. The letters were based on this principle withdrawn from him and given to the Administrator-General. The same principle was applied in the Estate of Nwana Francis Galega[26]. Here, Nwana Gertrude, the widow,

---

[24] Suit No. HCK/AE/K.16/2000 (unreported).

[25] .Supra fn 18

[26] Appeal No. BCA/19/93 (unreported).

applied for letters of administration against which the defendant, Wonyonga Thompson Galega the brother of the deceased filed a caveat. In spite of the animosity between the parties, the trial court granted joint administration to the parties. The decision was reversed at appeal and the administration granted to the Administrator-General on the ground that neither of the parties could administer the estate in the best interest of the beneficiaries "without fanning the flames of animosity between the two families."

The facts showed that the brother of the deceased was hostile to the surviving spouse and children, while the widow was opposed to the inclusion of the deceased's dependent mother and two illegitimate children as beneficiaries. In granting administration to the Administrator General of Mezam the Court of Appeal held that:

> *"The terrible rift that exists among the two families is so serious that they could not help exhibiting it to the court during trial. They quarrelled before, after and even during court sessions. On the 27th July 1995 after we had just finished hearing this appeal and adjourned it for judgment, another incident occurred which made our blood boil..."*

Influence of choice of marriage (monogamy versus polygamy)

Problems of adaptability of received laws often arise. For instance, when the law talks of surviving spouse, the ideal is one widow or widower. Section 21 (1) above would easily apply to the widow who was monogamously married but where there is more than one widow, the tendency is to lean towards customary law. In Estate of Fosah,[27] there was a disagreement between the two widows of the deceased Agatha and Alice that the Administrator General had to administer for some years before partitioning the estate after the two widows could finally agree.

The status of two opposing widows will also be a determinant. For instance a widow who was legally married will be considered over a customary widow or a widow to a void marriage. A case in point is

---

[27] HCB/99m/88.

Estate of Njonchuit.[28] Here, the first widow who was customarily married and who claimed to have jointly acquired the estate with the deceased was passed over in favour of the second widow who was legally married. In the same regard, the Court of Appeal South West in *Sam Mbessa Mani Christine v. Sam Wanji Christine & Sam Evans Florain*[29] held that the second wife could not be regarded as the widow of the deceased since she was polygamously married in 1986 whereas the first widow had earlier been married monogamously to the deceased under the Marriage Ordinance.

Conflict of laws (The influence of customary law)

Section 27(1) of the Southern Cameroons High Court Laws 1955 provides that:

> "The High Court shall observe, and enforce the observance of every native law and custom which is not repugnant to natural justice, equity and good conscience or incompatible with any written law for the time being in force, and nothing in this law shall deprive any person of the benefit of any such native law or custom."

Succession under customary law is basically patriarchal and patrilineal though in very rare cases there is patrilocal succession where a female can succeed so long as she remains unmarried and stays in her father's compound as is the case with the Mafors of the Mankon chiefdom [30]. There is however fairly significant matrilineal succession in both the North West and South West Regions particularly amongst the Bakundus and Balues in the South West Region and the Kom, Aghem, Weh and Buh in the North West Region. Matrilineal systems venerate the woman and the reasons seem to be specific to each tribe.

---

[28] HCK/AEK/94.
[29] CASWP/43/2006 of 19 February 2009.
[30] A mafor is a princess who holds a title (usually a queen mother)

Three major reasons have been advanced for the unavoidable influence of customary law in cases of succession. Firstly, a man's personal law governs succession. The prevalence of ancestral worship and veneration of the dead according to this view make certain issues impossible to be dealt with by received English law, such as the designation of the traditional 'successor or chop chair" or access to a traditional stool. It should be noted that the administrator could be different from the traditional successor or chop chair.

Secondly, the application for the grant of letters is put in motion by the next-of-kin declaration, which is only obtained from the customary courts. Thus if in a matrilineal setting, for example, the family decides to disinherit the deceased's widow and children by choosing the deceased's nephew to inherit, should the nephew obtain a next-of-kin declaration and apply for grant of letter of administration, the High court will have no choice than to grant the letters. This is compounded by the fact that some judges in the Common Law courts carry a "customary conscience" involving issuing customary law decisions from the common law bench. As the saying goes, the law is only as good as the judge. Most judges and magistrates come from a customary background and in applying their "in time conviction" have sometimes issued repugnant decisions based on customary laws.

Maya Ikome v. Manga Ekemason[31] is an excellent illustration of this unfortunate situation. Here, the deceased woman and her husband had been married for thirty years and had even blessed their marriage in church. When upon her death the widower applied for a next-of-kin declaration, the deceased woman's family opposed it on the basis that they did not 'know' her husband as he had never paid bride price. The customary court dismissed their claim holding that there was evidence of marriage from the marriage certificate presented. Strangely enough, the South West Court of Appeal in setting aside the judgment of the customary court held that a marriage certificate is only 'prima facie evidence of marriage' and that since bride price was

---

[31] CASWP/CC/76/85 (unreported).

not paid the marriage certificate 'did not perfect what was already an imperfect union.' By this strange reasoning, the court of Appeal disinherited the surviving husband.**??**

Despite the prevalence of custom, the High Courts would in most cases apply the repugnancy rule and refuse to apply custom. A pertinent example is in the custom of the levirate which is contrary to section 77(2) of The 1981 Civil Status Registration Law. The South West Court of Appeal in *Elive Njie Francis v. Hannah Efeti Manga*[32] rejected the appellant's claim that, since by the Bakweri custom he had provided a sack cloth for the widow of his uncle, he had become the next-of-kin of the deceased and husband to the widow. This contention had also been rejected by the Bwenga Customary Court which named the widow as next-of-kin. It is in the same light that Ngassa J had in *David Tchakokam v Keuo Magdaleine*[33] held that:

"any custom which says that a woman or any human being for that matter is property and can be inherited along with a deceased's estate is not only repugnant to natural justice, equity and good conscience, but is actually contrary to written law."

In Estate of Ibue Nobonda,[34] a case of matrilineal succession, the daughter of the deceased obtained letters of administration but one Sakwe Adolf and three others who were grandchildren to the deceased's sister applied for the letters to be revoked. They (plaintiffs for revocation) claimed that upon their grandmother's divorce from their grandfather, the deceased, they refunded their grandmother's bride price. By so doing all the issue of that defunct marriage were cut off from their grandfather by tradition and the deceased Ibue adopted their fathers as his children. Strangely enough, the Meme High Court ruled in favour of Sakwe and three others (plaintiffs for revocation) and ordered the Kombone Customary court to partition the estate amongst all the beneficiaries which included Disele Regina and all the plaintiffs for revocation. The same Kombone Customary

---

[32] (1999) Suit No. CASWP/cc/12/98).
[33] HCK/AE/K.38/97/92 ; 1999 G.L.R. 111.
[34] AE/K.25/2003-2004 (unreported).

Court that had granted her the Next-of-Kin Declaration partitioned the estate amongst Sakwe and others, leaving out Disele Regina. Disele Regina appealed. The Court of Appeal in CASWP/18/2008 quashed the decision of the court below on grounds that the court had granted reliefs not sought.

Inheritance rights of Married girls

The inheritance right of a married woman has been instituted and preserved in the case of Estate of Chibikom[35] the *locus classicus* in this province of the law in Cameroon. The appellant, a married woman was the oldest child of the deceased. She applied and was granted letters of administration, which like the next-of-kin declaration, were supposed to be provisional. After some years of administration, her brothers were dissatisfied with the grant of letters and brought an action for its revocation. Having failed in the High Court, they appealed to the North West Court of Appeal which revoked the letters and holding that "it is common ground that the respondent, a married woman, belonged to a different family and could not inherit from her father in accordance with customary law."

Undeterred Zamcho Florence appealed to the Supreme Court which quashed the decision of the lower court noting that:

"Not only was the decision of their learned lordships based on sex discrimination in gross violation of the contents of the preamble of the constitution, but it was in total misrepresentation of section 27 of the Southern Cameroon High Court Law which ensures the observance of the native law and custom only on the sole condition that it is neither repugnant to natural justice, equity and good conscience nor incompatible either directly or by implication with any law in force in the Republic, that they applied the so called principle of native law and custom which sustained a discrimination based on the sex of individuals."

---

[35] *Zamcho Florence Lum v. Chibikom Peter Fru &Others*, Supreme Court judgment No. 14/L of 14 Feb. 1993.

The position of children born out of wedlock:

One would have thought that with the country's strict marriage laws, children born out of wedlock will be treated differently when it comes to property settlement. However, case law developed by the courts tends to protect the rights of illegitimate children. In Re Estate of Nwana Francis [36] one of the reasons why the widow was not given sole administration over her deceased husband's estate was because of two illegitimate children whose rights, the court felt, she would not protect. Subsequently, In the Estate of Nana, [37] Ngassa J. ruled that there are no illegitimate children, only illegitimate parents.

Administration of Estates

Administration which refers to the period during which the estate is realized and prepared for liquidation, commences from the death of the deceased to the time estate is distributed. Administration is carried out by the deceased's 'personal representative' who is normally the nearest relative or next-of-kin. The personal representative manages the estate on behalf of the beneficiaries, who are persons entitled to maintenance by the deceased either directly or by the proxy of those in whose favour the right existed

The administrator or personal representative is like a liquidator. The duties of the administrator are almost akin to those of an executor under a will. He/she does not own the property subject to the grant but only manages it for the benefit of the beneficiaries. The property cannot be attached for the administrator's debts as was shown in *Stella Nunga & 5 others v. Clara Kumbongsi & 4 Others.*[38] Here,

---

[36] BCA/19/93(unreported).
[37] (2005) Suit No. HCF/PROB/AE1/2001-2002 (unreported).
[38] Cameroon Common Law Report, Part 5, 189, 194.

the deceased who died intestate was survived by his widow and six children. The widow to whom letters of administration were granted borrowed money from the first respondent and was unable to repay. The first respondent, Clara Kumbongsi, brought an action at the court of first instance to attach the property and succeeded. In reversing the decision on appeal, Ekema C J noted that since "the late Nunga did not at his death, will the property in question to his wife, Helen Nunga. His property therefore became family property at his death" He thus concluded that "all the beneficiaries of the Nunga estate had an interest in the estate."

Distribution

Distribution is the act of apportioning property after the interim period of administration. The manner of devolution will depend on the category of surviving relatives. When there is a surviving spouse the entitlement of the other beneficiaries will be subject to what she or he gets.

Devolution to the surviving spouse

The surviving spouse is the person who was married to the deceased at the time of death. As a basic rule, the surviving spouse is entitled absolutely to the personal chattels, which are the content of the matrimonial home, so that the surviving spouse continues to live in familial environment.

After the personal chattels, whatever the spouse obtains out of the residuary estate will be subject to the entitlements of other beneficiaries. The surviving spouse has a life interest in half of the residue if there are surviving issues. If there are no issues but parent or brother or sister of the whole blood or their issue, the spouse takes half of the residue absolutely. In the absence of the above specified relatives, the spouse takes the entire residue absolutely. (See generally sections 46(1) (i) and 47(2) and (3) of the Administration of Estates Act 1925.)

61

The Administration of Estates Act 1925 makes no express provision for the widow's entitlement to the matrimonial home. If the home was owned jointly, it does not form part of the residuary estate since the surviving spouse is entitled to it by survivorship (here, the ante nuptial settlement will be very relevant). Resort could be had to The Intestate Estates Act 1952, the second schedule of which makes for the acquisition of the "dwelling house" by the surviving spouse, provided that the surviving spouse was resident therein at the time of death.

The rules of distribution appear complicated but can be clearly applied by the courts as need arises. However, practice has shown that distribution is not done. Most administrators no doubt confuse their roles with that of the traditional 'chop chair' and so, administer forever thereby treating the estate of the deceased as their personal property. The solution to the above abuse lies in revocation and or sanctions for wrongful administration.

Revocation of grant of probate and letters

Grants of probate and letters may seem conclusive but are not final or fatal, as the court has authority to revoke them as provided for by section 20 of the Judicature Act 1925 and section 17 (1) and (2)) Administration of Estates Act 1956.Put sections before the statute. Thus, even if a widow or other rightful beneficiary finds that someone else has obtained letters, all is not lost as the letters are not final. Where it appears to the court that probate or administration ought not to have been granted or was granted in error, the court may recall and revoke them. Probate may also be revoked on grounds that it was obtained by fraud upon the court, where the verdict was obtained in default or where a latter will or marriage by the testator after the will is discovered, or where the testator thought to be dead is subsequently proved to be alive. The additional grounds on which letters of administration may be revoked are:

- Where the grant was made in an irregular manner, for example, without citing the necessary parties, or was obtained surreptitiously,[39]

-Where the grant was made to the wrong person e.g., to a woman claiming to be the widow of the intestate but who has not been legally married to him[40] or to an illegitimate person claiming to be a relative,[41]where the administrator becomes of unsound mind or otherwise incapable of acting.

Liabilities and penalties for administration of estates

Even where letters are not revoked the widow and beneficiaries of an estate may bring an action against the administrator for the following:

1. Intermeddling with estates:

One intermeddles with an estate when he administers it without grant of probate or letters. Even an executor named in a will must first prove the will before administering the estate. Under Order 48 of the Supreme Court (Civil Procedure) Rules Cap 211 penalties for intermeddling with an estate include a fine of up to 50 pounds sterling or six months imprisonment. One who intermeddles with an estate is called "an executor de son tort[42]"

2. Mismanagement by duly appointed Executor or Administrator:

The same penalty as above applies in addition to criminal sanctions for misappropriation of proceeds of an estate. In the *People v. Atongfack Paul Ngu & 1 other*[43] the first accused, the son of the deceased by his first wife, was granted letters of administration of the estate of Ngu Takunju Jean Bernard. The first accused/administrator

---

[39] Ravenscroft v. Ravenscroft [1671]1 Lev.305, Trimlestown v. Trimlestown [1830]3Hagg.Ecc.243.)

[40] In b.Moore [1845]3Notes ofCas.601;In b.Langley[1851]2 Robert 407

[41] In b.Bergman [1842] 2 Notes of Cas. 22.

[42] Mbokam Nya Clarice v. Tchouinjan Andre & CDC put citation

[43] TM/545/05-06 (unreported).

proceeded to empty the deceased's savings account of the sum of sixteen million (16.000.000) francs which he shared with second accused his uterine brother, excluding all the other beneficiaries. Upon complaint by Ngune Marguerite Jeanette, one of the widows of the deceased and the Administrator General of Fako, the first and second accused were convicted for misappropriation and sentenced to four years' imprisonment each.

Conclusion

It has been shown that although the law for the most part grants and enforces women inheritance rights, factors such as the interplay between common law, national laws, pervasive customary laws and sometimes civil law makes this difficult. The impact of these multiple and at times conflicting systems has been described by one author as: "a legal cocktail [in which] judges have had to determine the proper law applicable to each given transaction."[44]

Inheritance remains one of the main ways by which women acquire landed property for wealth, business and development. In an era of globalization with dynamic evolution and harmonization of laws, there is an urgent need to discard archaic and obscure laws in favour of a concrete uniform and comprehensive law on succession. It is hoped that the proposed Family Code will provide a solution to this quagmire that women find themselves in. In the interim, gifts *inter vivos* as well as a will by a loving and conscientious ancestor remain the best medium of securing women's inheritance rights.

---

[44] Sylvia Tamale – "When Hens begin to Crow: Gender and parliamentary politics in Uganda" (1999).

Chapter Four

Exploring Women's Rights within the Cameroonian Legal System: Where do Customary Practices of Bride-Price Fit in?

Vera N. Ngassa

Abstract

Colonization came along with different civilizations, giving traditional rulers subordinate positions, which were seemingly adopted later by government after independence. The government instituted laws with unprecedented human rights for women, notably in the constitution and the Civil Status Registration Ordinance of 1981, which redefined marriage, paternity, bride-price and widowhood. These developments notwithstanding, the socio-legal status of the Cameroonian woman remains an uphill task, as the woman is often seen as a source of wealth subject to male domination.

This paper gives an overview of women's rights with regards to customs related to bride-price, which defines marriage, childbirth, paternity, widowhood and property. It defines custom in historical context, portraying it as the only government and religion of the people before colonization. The paper conceptualizes gender within the context of human rights and liberties particular to women because of their vulnerability. It focuses on customs relating to bride-price, especially, and discussed the impact of bride price on the dissolution of marriage, widowhood, the practice of levirate, ownership of property and the paternity of a child, which according to custom, depends on the payment of the bride. The paper concludes that since custom is made by man, whatever is made by man can be improved upon, modified or discarded.

Introduction

Prior to the advent of colonialism in Cameroon, as in most parts of Africa, the only government, law and religion were custom. Custom was created, enforced and maintained through the institutions of chieftaincy, family, kinship, clans and ancestral worship. Custom can be defined as a usage or practice of society, which by common adoption and acquiescence and by long and unvarying habit has become compulsory, and which has acquired the force of law in a given society. Customary law consists of the indigenous customs of traditional communities.

> ✦ *Every ethnic group in Africa has evolved its own discrete customary legal system of rules that are binding on its members. Unlike ordinary social habits and observances, the rules carry along with them local sanctions for their breach. For the most part, the rules are unwritten.*[45]

The context in which custom was developed made it not only vital but relevant. The pre-colonial days were perilous times characterized by tribal wars, fights to establish tribes, migration, slavery and slave trade, ritual killings and sometimes cannibalism. It is obvious that with little or no technology, in an age when traveling was mostly by foot (except in cases where the chief was carried on a palanquin), and with the workforce coming from within the family survival could only be ensured by dwelling in clans and family, and customary rules had to be developed to ensure order.

When the colonial masters came, they brought in a different civilization, government, laws and religion. There was a separation between customary law and colonial law, and custom was relegated to matters that dealt specifically with natives. Customary Courts were created and even had criminal jurisdictions. Traditional rulers, instead

---

[45] Akintunde O. Obilade, 1979, The Nigerian Legal System, Sweet & Maxwell, 1979p.83

of being the ultimate authority, now became subject to masters.

It should also be noted that during this period, ɑ somewhat diluted in the transfer of colonial rule. This ᵤₑ ₑₑₐᵤₛₑ certain practices which the white man considered barbaric were either outlawed, punished or willfully abandoned through the influence of Christianity. In some cases, the people themselves learned certain convenient habits and replaced old usages. For instance, the killing of twins in certain parts of Africa gradually stopped and the practice of burying chiefs with live slaves was abandoned. The mysticism that used to accompany certain dreaded diseases like smallpox evaporated when the Whiteman demystified it with a medical cure. Thus the customary law as it is today is a diluted version of its pre-colonial form.

Then came the period of the British and French Mandates after the Germans were defeated in the First World War. The British and the French brought in their laws and permitted native laws and customs only insofar as they were convenient to their rule. After independence, governments of the newly independent states sought to merge customs and received western laws. Upon independence, Cameroon recognized the institution of customary law. Ordinance No. 72/4 of 6th July 1974 (which has been amended by the 1989 law and Law No 2006/015 of 26th December 2006), in apportioning jurisdiction, left certain matters of status to customary law. Customary and Alkali Courts were equally instituted by Law Number 79 - 4 of June 29th, 1979 on the organization of the Customary and Alkali Courts in Anglophone Cameroon as well as Decree number 69/D.F/544 of December 19th 1969 on the organization of Traditional Jurisdictions in former East Cameroon (Civil Law Cameroon).

Along with independence came a wave of new Cameroonian laws and institutions with unprecedented human rights for women, notably The 1972 Constitution with the notion of equality for all persons regardless of religion race or gender, the adoption of French Law and English law in Matrimonial causes and Probate matters, the ɔ4/65 penal code which criminalized certain attitudes of sexuality, child marriage (marriage of girls less than 14) bride price, and family life, and finally, the Civil Status Registration. The 1981 Civil Status Registration Ordinance amends the 1968 law on marriage, a law which drastically redefined marriage and the notion of bride price, widowhood and paternity. Yet in spite of the woman's rights enshrined in our laws, and in spite of the talk of gender equality and non-discrimination, the struggle towards elevating the socio-legal status of the Cameroonian woman remains an uphill-task.

The fact remains that a woman, whether she be just a girl-child or a wife, is generally regarded as a source of wealth and subject of male domination and exploitation. That is to say, a man derives so much convenience and material benefit from dominating a woman. (Women act as housekeepers, cooks, water and wood fetchers, baby sitters, child bearers, extra labor in the man's cash crop farms, providers of subsistence food crops, extra income from bride-price, and when they are gainfully employed, additional income for the family.) For this reason, one of the greatest hindrances to the elevation of the woman's legal status is the fact that men are unwilling to give up a social structure that they find comfortable. It thus becomes a taboo to challenge the status quo. One of the woman's greatest problems is the application of customary laws to the legal status of women in contradiction to the direction of the law and to social reality.

The reason often given to justify custom is that it is somehow in the best interest of society. This line of reasoning has often been invoked to deny women certain rights. Custom is not the only factor against women's rights. Other factors in our present social structure range from the law itself, lack of necessary laws on pressing issues, inability to enforce already enacted laws, the refusal of society to assimilate and exploit new laws, ignorance, legal illiteracy, poverty, and compromise of the woman herself. One thing, however, remains clear: while the law pretends to be gender neutral, custom is very gender sensitive.

Customary Laws and Practices as a Hind
Rights

The Nature of customary law

There are 250 ethnic groups in Cameroon with diverse ╲
but the following common threads run through the fabric
Cameroon customary laws:

- The present customary laws in Cameroon are a hybrid of custom and the influence of colonialism, Christianity, Islam or some other religion.

- Customary law is not written but passed down from generation to generation by oral tradition. Because it is transmitted orally from generation to generation, customary law contains a margin of error that makes it impossible to achieve the same level of clarity and precision frequently sought in Western legal concepts.[46]

- Customary law is therefore not static. Like any system of unwritten law, customary law has a propensity to adapt itself to new circumstances and changing times such as changes in the economic, political and social environment. For instance, bride price used to be paid in labor, and then in dowries, then in pounds and shillings, next in Franc CFA, and now in dollars.[47]

- In all customary systems, be they patriarchal or matrilineal, women have a status lower than that of men and are often equated to children and minors.

Customary laws and practices are applicable in our Common Law courts by virtue of section 27 of the Southern Cameroons High Court Law 1955, the Magistrates Court Law and, section 18(1)(a) of the Native Courts Ordinance, Cap. 142 of the 1948 Laws of Nigeria.

Section 27 (1) of the 1955 Law provides:

---

[46] T. W. Bennett and T. Vermeulen, 'Codification of Customary Law,' *Journal of African Law* Vol. 24, 1980, p. 206.
[47] See E. Cotran and N.N. Rubin, *Readings in African Law*, p. xix, 1970

"The High Court shall observe, and enforce the observance of every :ative law and custom which is not repugnant to natural justice, equity and good conscience or incompatible with any written law for the time being in force, and nothing in this law shall deprive any person of the benefit of any such native law or custom."

Furthermore, section 27(2) of the Southern Cameroon High Court Law 1955 empowers the courts to administer

"....such native law and custom as shall be deemed applicable in cases and matters where the parties thereto are natives and also in causes and matters between natives and non-natives where it may appear to the courts that substantial injustice would be done to either party by a strict adherence to the rules of English law."

⚐ The same principle applies in Civil Law Cameroon, where any customary law which is contrary to the notion of the "Ordre Publique" or "bonnes Moeurs et Ordre Publique" shall not be enforced[48]. Law Number 79 - 4 of 29th June 1979 on the organisation of the Customary and Alkali Courts in Anglophone Cameroon as well as Decree No. 69/D.F/544 of 19th December 1969 on the organisation of Traditional Jurisdictions in former East Cameroon (Civil Law Cameroon) both insist that the courts shall apply the customs of parties which are not contrary to the law and public policy. Worthy of note is the fact that in Cameroon, Islam is applied not as Sharia law but as customary law. Muslim law is applied and administered not by ordinary customary courts, but by the Muslim Alkali Courts.[49]

---

[48] See the case of Bebey Ekoume CI Marie EBENYE (1979) REVUE Camerounaise de droit 366,371 and Ministere Public C/ Andre (1975) RC.D342,345

[49] Law Number 79 - 4 of 29th June 1979 on the organisation of the Customary and Alkali Courts in Anglophone as read with s.27 Southern Cameroons High Court laws 1955

It follows from the above that there ought not to be any tussle between customary practices and the law but where there is a contradiction between custom and statutory law, then the latter ought to prevail. However, the reality of the day shows that custom and the modern law are vying for supremacy. This could be explained by the fact that people are first born into a family and a clan and are first introduced to custom before they are introduced to the laws of the state. Laws which contravene custom will be hard to enforce. This paper will be limited to women's rights vis a vis the most obvious customs which are customs related to bride-price for bride price invariably defines marriage, child birth and paternity, widowhood and property.

Bride-Price and the Validity of Marriage

Section 70 (1) of the Civil Status Registration Ordinance 1981 provides that the payment or nonpayment of bride price shall have no effect on the validity of marriage. In practice bride-price is still the be all and end all of marriages under the customs of tribes in Cameroon. The position succinctly put is this: *does this still hold?*

- No Bride price, no marriage
- Where bride price has been paid, there is a marriage, which subsists so long as it is not refunded.
- No refund of bride price, no dissolution of marriage

Thus we find that grown women are afraid to get married without the consent of their parents and some women divorce their husbands on the grounds of bride price. Besides, some Civil Status Registrars refuse to celebrate marriages simply on grounds that bride price has not been paid to the bride's father even if all relevant formalities and considerations have been fulfilled. Other adult couples who are legally married, suffer under the misapprehension that the wife's family has a right to break up the marriage if they have not been fully paid the bride price. Furthermore, sections 61 (1) and 70 (2) of the Civil Status Ordinance, which both forbid objections or actions brought against a marriage on grounds of the payment or non-payment on grounds of public policy, are completely ignored.

The most perturbing instances are when our modern Law courts, which are supposed to apply the written law, equity and good conscience, bow to customs that are incompatible with public policy and against the written law. In Maya *Ikome v. Manga Ekemason,* [50] the deceased woman and her husband had been married for thirty years and had their marriage blessed in church. Upon her death, her husband, the widower, applied for administration her property. The family of the deceased opposed, claiming that they did not know her to be married because bride price was not paid. The customary court dismissed their claims and held that there was evidence of marriage from the marriage certificate. In setting aside the judgment of the court below, the South West Court of Appeal held that the marriage certificate "is only prima facie evidence of marriage" and that since bride-price was not paid, the registration of the marriage evidenced by the marriage certificate, the blessing of the marriage in church, and the subsequent act of living together as man and wife by the parties for thirty years "did not perfect what was already an imperfect union." The Court of Appeal thus disinherited the widower/appellant and gave the deceased's property back to her family, thereby trampling where the customary court had feared to tread.

[handwritten marginal note: but this was reversed by Supreme Court...]

Bride-Price and Monogamy (and Bigamy)

Under Section 49 of the Civil Status Registration Ordinance, polygamy is an option but not obligatory. Monogamy is also a choice and a man commits the offence of bigamy under section 359 of the Penal Code 1965 if in being monogamously married, he unlawfully takes on a second wife before the dissolution of the monogamous marriage. However, the decision of the High Court of Fako in

---

[50] CASWP/CCI76/85 (Unreported)

Motanga v. Motanga [51] gives the impression that the Cameroonian man is free at any time to contract a polygamous marriage. Even if a man opts for monogamy, there is no guarantee that he will not one day relapse into polygamy. The payment of bride-price creates an unequal status for the woman.

A practice particular to Anglophone Cameroon, which makes nonsense of monogamy at the end of the day and creates a good excuse for bigamy, was developed from uncertain pedigree but may be traced to Section 49 of the Civil Status Registration Ordinance in 1981. Section 49 provides that apart from the type of marriage, the couple provide the 'property settlement' agreed upon. The problem is that early Civil Status Officers and Secretaries, who were mostly customary court clerks, were not legally trained and therefore did not understand the notion of community or separation of property. They made it a duty to ask the couple if bride price had been complied with and wrote that down on the marriage certificate. Under the entry: "Type of ante nuptial settlement:" they would enter: "according to the native laws and customs."[52] = polygamy..

A series of decisions from the Courts of Appeal declared that "Monogamy according to native laws and customs" is polygamy, as our native laws and customs know no notion of monogamy. In the leading case of *Kumbongsi v. Kumbongsi*,[53] the appellant, who had three other customary law wives apart from the respondent, sought to rectify a marriage certificate he had mistakenly signed with the respondent opting for 'monogamy with joint property." Ekema, C.J. ✻ ruled that "A man is either polygamously married or monogamously married but not the two forms simultaneously. This section shows the confusion of the courts on the issue of "property settlement– according to native laws and customs.

In *Tufon v. Tufon* , Suit No. HCB/59/MC/83. Asu, J held

"The inference is that what the parties stated as the marriage, i.e. Native

[51] HCB/2/76.

[52] The first training of Civil Status Registrars was done by FIDA Cameroon in 1998.

[53] CASWP/4/84 (unreported).

Laws and Customs of Kom people was what they intended. The insertion of the word 'monogamy' is therefore absurd."[54]

Monogamy, according to native laws and customs, is "nothing short of a wanton contradiction"[55] The offshoot of the above is that, in the event of trouble or litigation arising from such a marriage, the marriage is declared polygamous and the parties are referred to the customary courts. If the above position were to be followed, then no Cameroonian woman could aspire to a monogamous marriage because almost all Cameroon weddings are either preceded by or followed by the payment of bride price. The position has however improved by case law [56] and training of Civil Status Registrars and Secretaries. In the 1990s, successive High Courts began to rule that the words "according to native laws and custom were superfluous and did not affect the status of monogamous marriages. One such decision is *Nana v. Nana.* Also in 1996 (FIDA)[57] an Association of women jurists, trained all Civil Status registrars and Secretaries in the North West and South West on human rights, on the application of the Civil Status Ordinance and on the meaning of the words on a marriage certificates. Having understood what 'property or ante nuptial settlement' means, the registries have stopped inserting words about native law and custom or bride price.

Bride-Price and the Dissolution of Marriage

Section 77(1) of the 1981 Ordinance provides: "*in the event of death of one of the spouses or of a legally pronounced divorce, the marriage shall be dissolved.*" Under customary law, however, once

---

[54] The couple who had been customarily married many years before the registry marriage chose monogamy as the type of marriage and against the entry for "ante nuptial settlement "the civil status Registrar "According to the native laws and customs of the Kom people."

[55] See Family law in Anglophone Cameroon by E.N. Ngwafor p.39

[56] See for instance the decision of Ngassa J. in *Nana v. Nana* (2005) Suit No. HCF/PROB/AE1/2001-2002 (unreported).

[57] The Spanish acronym for International Federation of Women Lawyers

bride price has been paid on a woman, she becomes married to the man on whose behalf the bride price was paid. Even where a legal marriage does not ensue, she is still regarded as the wife of the man who paid her bride price.

In an event of divorce, native laws and custom of most tribes in Cameroon hold that where a married woman obtains a divorce but does not refund the bride price, she remains married to the bride price payer for as long as the money is not refunded, no matter how many husbands she subsequently marries. Even when she dies, her corpse belongs to the man whose bride price she owes, and many legal or current husbands have been embarrassed and disgraced by traditional husbands seizing corpses on grounds that his bride price was not refunded. Even fathers of deceased wives have been known to seize corpses from hapless widowers on the grounds of non-payment of bride price.

Bride-Price has an important impact on widowhood. As earlier pointed out, by section 77 (1) of The Civil Status Registration Ordinance 1981, the death of a woman's husband dissolves the marriage, ends the relationship and any obligations that arose under it.

Section 77(2) goes further to provide:

"In the event of the death of the husband, his heirs shall have no right over the widow, nor over her freedom or the share of property belonging to her. She may, provided that she observes the period of widowhood of 180 days from the date of the death of her husband, freely remarry without anyone laying claim to whatever compensation or material benefit for dowry or otherwise, received either at the time of engagement, during marriage or after marriage."

If the above law were to be properly applied, then the widow has the following rights and freedom:
- Freedom from the bonds of the marriage to her deceased husband
- The right to a brief period of mourning (six months).

75

- The right to remarry.
- Freedom from (levirate marriage (having to marry any of the deceased's male relatives).)
  - Absolvement from returning the bride-price, and
  - The right to a share of the property.

However, in routine, customary and traditional practices are often applied in contravention of Section 77(2) of the Civil Status Registration Ordinance 1981. All over the country, widows fester under the yoke of oppression and are tortured in the name of widowhood rituals. This has been encouraged by the fact that nobody complains. In some cases, death is viewed with superstition and widows succumb to cruel and inhuman treatment for fear that if they resist, they might never be cleansed or they could be accused of having killed the deceased husband and a worse fate might follow them and their children. Interestingly enough, it is only widows or "Moukoussas" on whom bride price was paid who undergo this cleansing torture. Widows are often subjected to false imprisonment and extortion among other offenses, but because these widows do not seek redress, the arm of the law is staid.

The practice of levirate marriages is another violation of the rights of women associated with widowhood. The levirate marriage is the custom whereby when a man dies; his widow is expected to marry one of her deceased husband's relatives. If she refuses, she is chased off the deceased's property and forced to pay back the bride price. The practice is prevalent among the Grass-landers of the North West and Western Provinces but also exists amongst the Bakossis in Kupe Muanenguba and even the Bakweris in the Fako Division of the South West Region. Levirate marriage is founded upon the belief that because bride price is paid on the husband's behalf by his family, even when he dies, the family still has a lien on the woman. In some families, when the males die young, widows end up marrying up to three or four brothers. The practice of the levirate marriage is clearly contrary to Section 77(2) of the 1981 Ordinance and repugnant to natural justice.

76

Where the levirate marriage is practiced against the widow's will, it amounts to the offence of forced marriage contrary to section 3 56(1) of the Penal Code and it warrants a punishment of up to ten years imprisonment plus a fine of up to one million (1.000.000) FCFA. Among certain Bamileke tribes, since most corpses come from the city and the widow may escape soon after the burial, they have devised a practice of delaying the burial until the widow 'consummates 'her marriage with the new husband. This act amounts to rape under section 296 of the Penal Code. However, the courts hardly ever get to know of any of the cases because the widows refuse to complain.

In David Tchakokam v Keou Magdaleine[58] amongst other things, the plaintiff, David Tchakokam, sought an order of the court to force his levirate wife to return to him and sought a declaration that she had no claims over her late husband's property, which he had inherited along with her. The Kumba High Court, in dismissing the claim, ruled that it was "the most objectionable, repugnant and obnoxious action to have been brought before a Common Law court barely three years to the close of the twentieth century."

Bride-Price and Paternity

In spite of section 43 of the 1981 Ordinance, which clearly states that paternity must result from a direct blood relation between father and child and section 72 of the same Ordinance, which provides that bride price shall under no circumstance give rise to paternity, the concept of paternity in many customary communities in Cameroon remains tied to the payment of bride price. A woman seems to have no right over her own child. The child belongs to some man or another depending on whose bride price is currently paid on the mother's head.

Under the customary and traditional practices of most tribes in Anglophone Cameroon, the problem of bride price and paternity can

---

[58] (HCK/AE/K.38/97/92) 1999 G.L.R. 111

be examined in three different circumstances.

- If the mother has never been betrothed, the child belongs to her father, provided he equally paid bride price on the mother, because a man owns his wife, her children and all that belongs to them. The courts are plagued with many birth declarations where the father's name is actually the mother's father. If the mother is married, the child would belong to her husband only if he paid his wife's bride price. If he did not, then all her children belong to her father or some other man who had paid bride price on the woman.

- If the mother is divorced and has not yet refunded the bride price, then any children she has are regarded as belonging to her estranged husband, since his dowry is still on her head.

- Where the mother is a widow, she must refund her bride price, or all children born after her husband's death would still be regarded as the children of her deceased husband's family. Some widows go as far as giving their deceased husband's full names to children born many years after his death. In *Ngeh v. Ngome* [59] Paulina Mekang left her husband Ngome without returning her bride price. Many years later she entered into a union with Paul Ngeh and gave birth to twins. Ngome sought to claim the twins as his and the courts below granted his request. Gordon C.J., in quashing those decisions, held that the Appeals Officer had "allowed rules and regulations of native law and custom to have so enslaved him as to have caused him to close his eyes to biological and other realities."

The law, however, faces a damaging setback when modern law jurisdictions allow native laws and customs to take precedence over written law, equity, good conscience and common sense. One such case in point is *Affaire Mbeuchem C/ Joseph Yetchi Jean et Sanjo Julienne.* [60]

---

[59] 1963 West Cameroon Law Report page 32-33.
[60] TGI Douala, Jugement Civil Du 16 Avril 1990.

78

Sandjo Julienne and Mbeutcham Jean were married in France in 1965. Owing to problems and a breakdown of the marriage, Sandjo Julienne obtained a divorce against Mbeutcham. The judgment was, however, in default and she failed to notify Mbeutcham by serving it to him. Julienne subsequently married to Yetchi Jean in 1977. Eight children were born of the union. In 1987, Mbeutcham sought a decision of the court nullifying the marriage between Julienne and Yetchi. The judges of the Douala High Court did not only hold that Julienne's second marriage was bigamous, but went ahead to recognise Mbeutcham as the father of the eight children born of the union between Yetchi and Julienne.

It should be noted that the decision in Affire Mbeuchem cannot be reconciled with section 341 of the Penal Code. Anyone whose conduct has the result of depriving a child of evidence of his true parentage commits the offence of cloud on parentage, which is punishable with up to ten years imprisonment. In *Mary Ngem Kimbu and Thomas Ngong Kimbu v. The People,*[61] the first appellant and her father, the second appellant, who were charged with cloud on parentage insisted throughout the trial that Edward Ngong-Nassa was not" culturally and biologically" the father of children born of the marriage between Ngong-Nassa and Mary Kimbu, simply because Ngong-Nassa had failed to pay Mary Kimbu's bride price and as such was "unknown" to her father. Those assertions no doubt riled the trial judge O.M. Inglis into meting out the maximum sentence of ten years imprisonment against the appellants. What saved the appellants on appeal was the fact that, although they both changed the children's names and vocally disavowed, Ngong Nassa's name still appeared as father of the children in question.

Refund Of Bride-price

Sections 71 (1) and (2) of the Ordinance provide that during an engagement or betrothal, anyone who receives anything as bride-

---

[61] (1997) I CCLR page 115-125.

price should consider it as a deposit and if the marriage does not take place, the depository shall immediately return it. Thus, there should be no such thing as "eating and not vomiting" which is a common phrase parents use at the time of receiving the bride-price.

Section 73 goes further to instruct:

 ✱   *"In the event of dissolution of a marriage as a result of divorce, the person who received the dowry may be asked to pay back all or part of the dowry if the court feels that such a person is totally or partially responsible for the divorce."*

It flows from the provision above that only the person who received the bride price should be asked to return it, should he be found to have contributed to the divorce. The ex-wife should never be asked to return what she did not receive in the first place.

In *Emilia Mesonge v. Clement Ngalame,*[62] Justice Eyole Monono set aside as unconscionable a customary court decision which asked the appellant to pay back all her bride-price and all that had been spent on her during marriage. Her father was asked to refund only a little part. [63] Likewise, in *Buma v. Buma*[64], Monekosso J. did not only denounce the custom of the Baba II people in the North West Province, but also lamented that the bride-price had to be refunded in the event of a divorce, notwithstanding the duration of the marriage and services that the wife rendered in the course of the marriage.

In spite of the above decisions, the customary practice of asking for a return of the dowry continues, save perhaps when a man sends away his wife without just cause or breaks up the engagement. Only

---

[62] CASWP/CCI73/87 (Unreported)

[63] See also BCA/2CC/87 between *Bih Ngwa Theresia v. Che Patrick Munifor* where Che Patrick Munifor was claiming the balance of seventy Six thousand five hundred (76.500) francs as part of the bride-price. The Court of Appeal held that he should be happy with what she as ex-wife had already paid him because the court did not consider that Che Patrick was entitled to anything after all the services Bih Theresia had rendered him during the marriage.

[64] Appeal No. BCA/20/819 (unreported).

then is she free from returning the bride price.

There seems to be no hope of redemption for the woman, however, when she seeks redress in modern law jurisdictions and the judge, who ought to apply equity and good conscience as well as the written law, becomes an advocate for custom. One such decision was *Mary Ayaba Azwe v. John Ayaba Tebid* [65] where the South West Court of Appeal ordered the appellant to pay back her bride price assessed and fixed at three hundred thousand (300.000) FCFA plus costs of one hundred thousand (100.000) FCFA before her husband would allow her to collect her belongings from the matrimonial home. The judge in the case actually took cognizance of section 73 of the 1981 Ordinance but went ahead to rule that there was no evidence that the appellant's father had contributed to the divorce and, since she had willfully left the house of her own accord, she should pay[66].

Bride-price, women and property

In defiance to all our salutary laws in favor of women owning property, the customary law position is that once bride-price is paid on a woman she and all that she begets, including her children, become her husband's property and, as such property, cannot own property.

1. Property Rights upon Divorce.

The trend of decisions on managing property after divorce from Cameroonian courts is, to say the least, confusing. While one set of judges holds the notion of woman as property to be contrary to the written law and repugnant to natural justice equity and good

---

[65] CASWP/32/96 of 22nd January 1997.
[66] Some husbands do not stop short of asking for bride-price but go ahead to claim for expenses and kitchen utensils. Such was the case in *Mbaacha Gaius Ebande v. Elizabeth Neh Ebande*[66].The danger of such Court of Appeal decisions is that they become precedent and other judges are accustomed to consider them good law.

conscience, the other set of judges subscribe vehemently to customary law and are unwilling to apply the written law. A case in point is the infamous decision in *Rose Ndollo Achu v. Richard A. Achu*[67] The appellant Rose Ndollo Achu, who was gainfully employed, was able to show that she had received a huge compensation for a work-related injury, which she gave to her husband to invest. Also when her husband was paying for the construction of the house, she took care of the children and household expenses and after work, carried water and molded mud bricks for the house. Yet his Lordship O.M. Inglis J had this to say:

> *"Here customary law does not countenance the sharing of property especially landed property, between, husband and wife on divorce. The wife is still regarded as part of her husband's property. That conception is underscored by the payment of dowry upon marriage and on the refund of the same on divorce."*

In some cases, the Court of Appeal has even trampled where the customary courts themselves failed to tread: In *Ngitedem Etienne v. Tashi Lydia*[68], the Customary Court actually awarded the wife one of two houses that she helped to build (an uncompleted house) and some household articles. The husband appealed. The North West Court of Appeal held that the Customary Court had no jurisdiction to share property especially landed property upon divorce and that no equity could apply in the circumstances. The Court of Appeal accordingly set aside the Customary Court order awarding the house to the woman.

2. Inheritance

The area of succession and inheritance is another area in which custom has wrestled with the written law. If a man dies intestate, Section 21(1) of the Non Contentious Probate Rules of 1954 sets the order of priority for grant of administration is as follows:

a) The surviving spouse;

---

[67] BCA/62/86 of Monday 20th June 1988
[68] BCA/46/86 (unreported)

b) The children of the deceased or the issue of any such child who has died during the life time of the deceased;

c) The father or mother of the deceased;

d) Brothers and sisters of the whole blood, or the issue of any deceased brother or sister who has died, brother and sisters of the half blood or their issue, grandparents, uncles and aunts of the whole or their issue, and ends with uncles and aunts of the half blood or their issue.

In practice however, the grant of administration is influenced by customary law considerations. The influence of customary law is unavoidable because, first, succession is governed by a man's personal law. Secondly, the grant of letters of administration is put in motion by the next-of-kin declaration, which is only obtained from the customary courts, and thirdly, some judges in Anglophone Cameroon still have what is known as a "customary conscience." Many magistrates and judges in Cameroon were born and raised by customary and traditional practices. This background seems to influence their psyche in court. When presiding over cases with issues involving customary and traditional practices, the tendency is to grant letters of administration to brothers and nephews of the deceased over the widow and children of the deceased and the girl-child has no place either in her father's or in her husband's estate.[69] In *the Estate of Noumbissie*[70]for instance, letters were granted to a cousin of the deceased. It is only after he had mismanaged the estate to the detriment of the first widow that the letters were revoked and given to the Administrator-General.

In *Estate of Chibikom (Zamcho Florence Lum v. Chibikom Peter Fru & Others,*[71] the Bamenda Court of Appeal, in revoking letters of administration granted them to a married daughter of the deceased who died intestate, stated that:

---

[69] An Example is *Maya Ikome v. Manga Ekemason* Supra note 6.

[70] (1985) Suit No. C.A.S.W.P/CC/16/85 (unreported).

[71] Supreme Court judgment No. 14/L of 14 February 1993.

"It is common ground that the respondent at all times material to these proceedings was and is still a married woman. She belongs to a family different from the one in which she was born. She cannot inherit from her father in accordance with customary law, and a fortiori she cannot be her father's next of kin. The respondent was doubtless aware of her disability when she applied to the Mankon Customary Court for a declaration of temporary next of kin."

It is only on appeal to the Supreme Court that the judgment of the North West Court of appeal was overturned. The Supreme Court, which quashed and annulled the decision of the lower court, pronounced as follows:

"Not only was the decision of their learned lordships based on sex discrimination in gross violation of the ... contents of the preamble of the constitution, but it was in total misrepresentation of section 27 of the Southern Cameroon High Court Law which ensures the observance of the native law and custom only on the sole condition that it is neither repugnant to natural justice, equity and good conscience nor incompatible either directly or by implication with any law in force in the Republic, that they applied the so called principle of native law and custom which sustained a discrimination based on the sex of individuals."

The case has become a *cause célèbre* for having instituted female succession in customary law in Cameroon, but female children still struggle with their male sibling for access to their fathers' property. The tussle continues, and as author Mbua Alexander Assanga put it, "If the legislator thought he had buried bride price, it is still ruling us from the grave"[72]. This is because even when laws change, discrimination persists and actual change is often incrementally implemented.

The conflict between custom and the law ought not to exist

---

[72] "The Legal Perspectives of Bride-price" (ENAM dissertation 1987)

because, in principle, whenever custom differs from the law, then the written law ought to prevail. The power of custom, however, is the fact that it has been handed down to us by our ancestors and that there is a lot of ancestral worship and reverence in Cameroon. Many wives or ex-wives and their families succumb to customary practice of returning the bride-price simply because they want to avoid problems with the ex-husband and his family, especially when they had children. The idea is that by returning the bride-price to the ex-husband, it will create a peaceful atmosphere between the two families and the children can live in harmony with both families. The tests of every tradition should nevertheless still be the tests of reasonableness, equity and good conscience. [Ekome suggests that this paragraph should be part of the conclusion.]

Conclusion

From the above it would appear that the march towards gender equality seems to be taking us one step forward and two steps back. Times have changed and we can no longer apply pre-colonial rules and methods in a post millennium era. We must change with the times. The world has become a global village and with international conventions, our practices in our countries are no longer our private and sovereign business but they have become a matter for international concern. What we do in Cameroon can be seen by satellite and shown on the internet. Cameroon has ratified many human rights conventions one of which is the Convention on the Elimination of all forms of Discrimination Against Women. Cameroon is under international obligation to eradicate all customs and practices which contradict international norms. [73]

In an age where words like "networking, partnership, cooperation, and best practices "have become household words, if

---

[73] See 2006 UN recommendations on the subject especially Fact Sheet No.23, Harmful Traditional Practices Affecting the Health of Women and Children available at
http://www.wunrn.com/news/2006/02_19_06/022206_harmful_traditional.htm

the scope of laws have become wide enough to accommodate and include custom, custom can be wide enough to accommodate the law. Indeed history will show that many customs have been modified, discarded or simply forgotten. In fact, the notion of family property has completely changed as property is no longer communally held but rather individuals from families hold individual and private property. Women are now educated and earn incomes sometimes higher than those of their husbands. Some have become breadwinners of the family, sponsoring children and owning landed property.

The subject of women's rights can never be handled from one angle or perspective. In the words of Mary Robinson the former United Nations Commissioner for Human Rights, we must adopt 'an inter-disciplinary holistic approach.'[74] There is a customary approach to human rights and a human rights approach to custom waiting to be birthed.

---

[74] Message from the High Commissioner for Human Rights on the occasion of the 50th anniversary of the Universal declaration of Human Rights

Chapter Five

Women and Land Registration in Anglophone Cameroon: Lessons from South Africa

Michael A. Yanou & Patience Sone

Abstract

The Anglophone region of Cameroon has a significant problem of inequality in land holding between men and women. This paper reviews the land registration mechanism in the region in the context of this inequality of the landholdings between the sexes, which has resulted in a situation where over 80% of the registered lands in the region are in the hands of men. After identifying the Land Consultative Board as the principal body dealing with land registration, the paper criticizes it for consolidating patriarchal rules of land ownership. It argues that the prominent role given to the chief and two notables in the Board who are generally committed to customary law is a major obstacle inhibiting women from registering land on equal footing with men. The Supreme Court of Cameroon was also criticized for giving credence to the notion of ancestral property in *Ekolena Fouda Jean Inheritors v The State of Cameroon (MINDA)* because the concept strengthens patriarchy.

It has, in this paper, been demonstrated that the land registration law in Cameroon is similar to that of South Africa, as both have been used to achieve the exclusion of certain segment of society from owning land. Just as Section 5 of the Glen Gray Act was used to stop Africans whose lands had been dispossessed during apartheid from rebelling to get back their land, section 12 of Decree No 76/166 of April 1976 is used to give the chief and his two notables in the Board a strong voice to protect customary rules that restrict women's rights to own property. The difference between the South African situation and that of Cameroon is, according to this paper, very minor. While in South Africa race was the basis of exclusion during apartheid, sex is the basis of discrimination in Cameroon to date.

Introduction

The main theme of this paper is the land registration process in Cameroon with particular emphasis in the Anglophone regions. The paper timely calls attention to the worrisome fact that most Cameroonians, including the government, seem to take the centrality of land as a resource for survival and security of the individual for granted. This attitude is partly connected to the much wider phenomenon associated with the casual assumption that land disputes do not raise human rights concerns since land law and human rights are not natural bedfellows. This view assumes that human right stresses concern for the other person, while land law, which is opposed to this idea, is concerned with the notion of personal appropriation with its tendencies to exclude others[75].

The above conceptualization invariably causes government and policy-makers not to take the issue of the limited access to land by women seriously. However, lessons in Cameroon and elsewhere have demonstrated that this view is fundamentally erroneous. Indeed according to Leroy,[76] the Commission on Human Security (2003) had identified competition over land and resources as the number one cause of internal conflicts in Africa. It is obvious that the preponderate majority of inter – community/village wars are land-driven in the North West Region of Cameroon.

---

[75] Gray, K. (2002) 'Land Law and Human Rights,' in Tee, I., *Land Law: Issues, Debates, Policy,* Devon: William Publishing 211.
[76] Leroy, M. *Environment and Conflicts in Africa Reflections on Darfur.* Addis Abba: University for Peace, 2009 p51.

This same trend was graphically captured in South Africa by Letsoalo (1987)[77] who had noted that whatever minor causes there may have been for the many Bantu European Wars in the country, the competition for land was at the root of these wars. Although the general tendency is to interpret this competition and resultant violence over land in the context of the struggle between different communities over land, a comprehensive review of the phenomenon shows that there are a variety of different strands in this conflict. This paper reviews the land registration process in Anglophone Cameroon in the context of the strand that stresses the struggle over land between men and women, which has resulted in the bulk of registered lands being in the hands of men.

Theoretical framework of the paper

The paper situates the subject of women and land registration within Locke's theoretical conception of the equality of human beings. Locke believed that it was possible to tie the right to property (land inclusive) to the two social compacts concluded by individuals as people left the imperfect state of nature.[78] According to this view, the first social compact saw people joining together in a civil society while the second involved the establishment of a government with political power to protect their rights. The acquisition of property is, from Locke's theoretical standpoint, predicated on the fact that "the earth and all inferior creatures be common to all men," with everyone having a right to whatever they mixed their labor with.[79] It is, from this theoretical perspective, obvious that a woman ought to have ownership rights over land that she has possessed and used over time, including the power to register it in her name.

---

[77] Yanou M A, *Dispossession and Access to Land in South Africa: An African Perspective.* Bamenda: Langaa (2009) pg 20.
[78] See John Locke *The Second Treatise on Civil Government and A Letter of Toleration* (eds) in J W Gough Oxford Basil Blackwell (1948) 4-6.
[79] Locke op cit at 15.

The study also raises the illumination theory of property as right that concentrates on describing land by reference to a bundle of abstract rights. Although this theory is particularly English, it does have significant resonance in the context of Anglophone Cameroon for two reasons. The region inherited a common law tradition from England, which colonized it as a mandate territory before independence and unification with the former East Cameroon. Situating the paper in the context of this theory is appropriate because the current property paradigm in Cameroon recognizes different property rights and interests. Thus, customary law recognizes ancestral property as an interest in land in the same way that legislation recognizes the land certificate.

Social welfare Component of Land

The paper is also based on the social welfare theory, which stresses the adoption of land use options that will lead to a redistribution of land to attain social welfare objectives such as the fight against poverty and the provision of greater security of insecure tenures[80]. The social welfare component of land has been studied mostly by sociologists and anthropologists and is concerned with the impact of land use on the individual, family and community. The argument in this paper that the Cameroonian land policy essentially ignores this welfarist approach by failing to respond to the needs of the majority of women who do not own land is structured within the welfarist conceptualization of property.

African World view on property rights

A theoretical discourse on land in Cameroon would be incomplete without reference to the African continent's world-view

---

[80]T. Allen, *The Right to Property in Commonwealth Countries*. Cambridge: Cambridge University Press (2000):202.

as well. Fisiy[81] notes that African societies did develop an ethical system under which ownership, control and management of land are defined. However, because decisions in ancient African communities were arrived at by consensus and because the community was not driven by a desire for profit or wealth, collective resources were distributed in accordance with individual needs. This political mechanism for distributing benefits translated into each individual member of society having rights to goods and services on the basis of need.[82] This African perspective seeks to give content to the overriding idea of human dignity as it guarantees the provision of the needs for dignified living.

It is from this theoretical perspective argued that Cameroonian customary rules which limit women's right to own property, are a product of a colonialist misunderstanding of ancient African legal notions. This misunderstanding has resulted in the failure to appreciate the basic rights developed under indigenous systems prevailing in pre-colonial Africa. It is obvious that belief in the powers of ancestral spirits and their intervention in the day to day affairs of the living, which are prevalent in almost all African traditional societies were meant for the good of men and women alike. Unfortunately this belief system, which has been distorted by those driven by profit, now shapes the African's conception of his relationship to the community and forms part of the positive morality which influences the way law operates in African societies in the same manner that most European legal rules are connected to Judeo-Christian origins.[83]

---

[81] C F Fisiy, Power and Privilege in the Administration of Law: Land Law Reforms and Social Differentiation in Cameroon. Leiden Africa Studies Centre (1992):1.
[82] See T. Bennett, 'The Compatibility of African Customary Law and Human Rights' (19991) Acta Juridica:30
[83] Fisiy op cit at 1 & 6.

Research Methodology

This study adopted qualitative, quantitative and empirical methodologies. The qualitative component of the study shall involve a content analysis of primary and secondary data in order to identify the impact of land registration on land ownership by women in Anglophone Cameroon. It reviews such primary data as legislation and case law relating to land registration in the region. The study involved the content analysis of secondary data from government policy documents and reports, academic journals and books. This entailed an extensive review of journal articles, reports, government publications and books on land access and land registration in Cameroon. There was also a desktop research done to gather information from government departments in charge of land tenure promotion. The information collected from these departments was supplemented by reports obtained from surveys on land registration carried out by other organizations within the country. This extensive literature review helped to identify the various land registration traits in the country and the reforms put in place to mitigate the negative effects of land inaccessibility for women.

The quantitative component of this study entailed a limited field visit for data collection. A structured questionnaire was developed to determine the prevalence of certain acknowledged land registration traits within the various communities in Anglophone Cameroon and how these affect women. The data on land holdings was collected mainly from the land registries in the delegations of State Property and Land Tenure in the region under review. A total of about 500 questionnaires were administered.

Land and Registration: An Overview

Typically, land registration refers to the keeping of public records of all transactions involving land, a practice[84] which dates back many centuries. Although this definition is standard and apparently reflects what obtains in practice, it does on a circumspect review appear clearly deceptive. In reality, land registration has not always been driven by altruistic objectives nor has it been designed to achieve equal access to land between men and women. The experiences in Cameroon and South Africa have shown that the registration process has not been exclusively used to map and capture existing legal rights in land as the above standard definition appears to suggest at face value.

The actual registration process in Cameroon is managed by the Land Consultative Board as stipulated in article 16 of Law No 74/1 of 6th July 1974, generally called "the 1974 Land Ordinance." The Board is the most important statutorily created administrative structure in the country's land management model. Presided by the divisional officer[85], the Board operates under the supervisory control of the Minister of Land and State Properties with exclusive powers for land acquisition and distribution in the country. Although the Board is a purely administrative body[86] made of government officials, a traditional authority (the village chief) and two notables in the area of coverage sit in the Board.

It is apparent that the Board plays a crucial role in the registration process and, by extension, in land distribution,[87] although its conclusions are technically regarded as recommendations in the form of advice to the Minister of Lands, which he is not, obliged to take.

---

[84] D. Watcher & Eylich J The World Bank Experience with Rural Land Titling WB Working Pyler (1992)35.

[85] Article 12 Decree No. 76/166 of 27/4/76 as amended in 1985.

[86] The Board only has competence to make recommendations to the minister of land under Law No 76/166 of 27/4/76.

[87] The Board is the body that determines the authenticity of the spatial apportionment of land for and on the behalf of the minister of land. This is what, in practice, determines the current land holding in the country.

Few recommendations on whom to issue a land certificate are, in practice, disregarded by the Minister. The view of the Board has, in fact, currently become stronger since the process for issuing land certificates was decentralized in 2007.

It has, in a recent study,[88] been demonstrated that the land registration process is underpinned by customary law rules that exclude women from owning land. The argument in the study that the registration process consolidates patriarchal rules of land ownership to the disadvantage of women is indisputable, considering the Boards depend hugely on the advice of two of its members, who are traditional rulers and notables and whose commitment to customary rules of patriarchy remains unshakable. Sone's[89] study shows that the situation has not significantly changed in 2011 from what it was over two decades ago when Fisiy[90] had, in an earlier work, noted that the registration process is customary law-driven. The latter had, in his research, stated that the practice of the Board reinforced the argument that land is acquired under customary law and registered under state law!

Quite clearly, the practice of issuing land certificates on the basis of a registration process in Cameroon that is predicated on customary law rules of exclusion must be condemned for its potential to consolidate discrimination against women with regards to their access to land. This is all the more so considering, as article 1 of the 1974 Land Ordinance and the decision in *Max Ntangsi V Pangoup*[91] insisted, that the land certificate is absolute and indefeasible.[92] In spite of the decision in Ntangsi's case, the overwhelming dominance of custom and tradition in ultimately determining land distribution in the country can be deduced from the apex court on disputes over land.

---

[88] P. Sone, The Concept of Equality and Access to land in Cameroon: The case of Anglophone Regions of Cameroon PhD thesis Department of Law, University of Buea (2011).

[89] Sone op cit at 4.

[90] Sone Op cit at (3) Judgment Number 50/06-07 of 28th February 2007.

[91] CASWP/11/2002.

[92] Land certificates may, however, be withdrawn as was done supreme Court in Ekolena Jean inheritors Vs The State of Cameroon (Supra).

The jurisprudence of the administrative bench of the Supreme Court, which is the highest arbitral body over land, established the principle that the land registration process accommodates customary law discriminatory rules of access to the extent of compromising land certificates issued by the state.

In the case of *Ekolena Fuoda Jean inheritors Vs the State of Cameroon (MINDA)*[93], the petitioner sought the cancellation of a land certificate for a variety of reasons, particularly that the land was the "ancestral property" of the petitioner. The claims of the petitioner were declared admissible and the land certificate was withdrawn by the Supreme Court. It is particularly instructive that the court recognized and expressly gave credence to the concept of ancestral property.

It must be observed that the idea of ancestral property both in Cameroon as well as elsewhere, denotes the idea of property within a group that is usually made up of the dead, the living and the yet unborn. This notion, in effect, results in the view that ancestral property should be controlled by men who perform the ritualistic roles in their capacity as the medium for communication between the living and the ancestors. It is this customary conception of land, the role of male heads, etc. that are responsible for the lopsided land holding in favor of men in Cameroon.

Registration as Instrument for Exclusion: South African Experience

Land registration in South Africa dates back to 1894 when the Glen Grey Act was enacted. Like in Cameroon land registration in South Africa is an essentially foreign phenomenon. This Act was quite plainly unconcerned with the mapping and capturing of interest on land, despite how it appeared to suggest. Section 5 of the Act governing the registration process was to this extent instructive for making registration of transferred land subject to the approval of the governor (who was, by the rules of apartheid, white). Interestingly,

---

[93] Supra

the provision also prescribed that registered land was subject to be forfeited for rebellion.

One did not need to be ingenious to see that section 5 of the Act was meant to protect apartheid's grand design aimed at the dispossession of indigenous Africans from their ancestral land. After using armed violence and trickery to seize African land, section 5 was designed and enacted to ensure that Africans do not rebel or fight to recover the land from which they had been dispossessed. Clearly, the Act was meant to weaken the resistance of Africans who had seen 80% of their land expropriated by an alien European settler community. It is for this reason that the African National Congress (ANC) had argued against the protection of land rights in the South African constitution in such a way that would fossilize past injustices.[94]

The Cameroonian experience in using legislation to accomplish a hidden agenda with regard to access of land is similar to what occurred in South Africa. The only difference, in fact, is minor. While in South Africa race was the basis for exclusion, in Cameroon, sex is used to deprive women from owning land. Section 12 of Decree No 76/166 of April 1976, which regulates the terms and conditions of management of national land, is the specific instrument of discriminatory access. The section demands the presence of 'the chief and two leading members of the village or the community where the land is situated' in the Land Consultative Board. Their dominant role in the Board and obvious patriarchal disposition as discussed earlier has produced a massively unequal land distribution pattern between men and women in the region as shown in the table below:

---

[94]Yanou M A op cit at 99.

Table 1: Summary of total number of applicants for land certificate in the Anglophone regions from January 1980 –June 2010.[95]

Applicants	Total Number of Applicants for Land Certificates from each region		Total number of Applicants in the Anglophone regions	Percentage
	North West Region	South West Region		
Men	6635	3692	10327	84.5
Women	572	859	1431	11.7
Joint Ownership	233	233	466	3.8
Total	7440	4784	12224	100

Table 2: Summary of land certificates acquired in the Anglophone regions from January 1980 – June 2010.[96]

Beneficiaries	Total Number of Acquired Land Certificates from each region		Total number of beneficiaries in the Anglophone regions	Percentage
	North West Region	South West Region		
Men	6630	3586	10216	86.6
Women	471	657	1128	9.6
Joint Ownership	220	232	452	3.8
Total	7321	4475	11796	100

---

[95] Information derived from both the North West and South West Regional Delegations of State Property and Land Tenure. Accessed on 5/08/2010.
[96] Ibid

97

The above tables reveal that, out of a general total of 12224 applications received for land certificate in the Anglophone regions from January 1980 – June 2010, 11,796 land certificates were issued. Out of the 11,796 land certificates, a total of 10,216 land certificates were issued in men's names, denoting a percentage of 86.6 land certificates controlled by men in the regions. Also, out of 11,796 land certificates granted, 1,128 of the land certificates were issued in women's names, giving a percentage of 9.6 land certificates controlled by women. While a total of 452 land certificates were issued as joint ownership to the applicants, giving a total of 3.8% land certificates controlled by the applicants. Hence, although fewer women applied for land certificates, more women were denied land certificate (303). While many men applied, few yet were denied land certificate (111). The present analysis is a clear demonstration that unequal access to land is still deeply entrenched in the Anglophone regions. Indeed, women presently own less than 10% of the total number of land certificates existing in the regions despite the fact that they are more involved in agricultural activities. Apart from graphically demonstrating the profound challenges women face in land ownership, the statistics confirm that the apparent gender neutrality of our land laws do not protect women adequately, as they allow customary practices to determine rules of land access to the disadvantage of women.

We cannot afford to have a Land Consultative Board with all male traditional authorities and notables and expect that the result of what they do will not protect past and present discrimination against women. In South Africa, both the decisions of courts and the making of express laws were influenced by the need to address the most enduring legacies of racism, namely the gross unequal distribution of land in the country. There is a need to do the same in Cameroon because a situation where men hold over 80% of the land in Cameroon is clearly similar to the South African colonial experience where whites held over 80% of the land. We contend that Cameroon's land registration regime, which is based on the idea of

98

formal equality, needs to, in practice, take account of the fact that women who are already discriminated against demand affirmative action to reverse the inequitable distribution of land in the country. Admittedly, the preambular provision of the Cameroonian Constitution 2008 prohibits discrimination on the basis of sex and the other usual idiosyncratic basis in the country. However, the above statistics show that this has not, in practice, translated to equal access to land for Cameroonian women. It is, in light of the above, necessary for the country to draw inspiration from South Africa where the country's Constitutional Court in *Government of South Africa v Grootboom*[97] concluded that a state in which any significant number of a vulnerable group (like women) has no access to land and housing is in breach of its minimum core obligation to protect its citizens under international law.

Conclusion

We have in this paper attempted to show that the land registration system in Cameroon is deliberately skewed in favour of men. The evidence is the fact that, although women are more in population and use land more for subsistence agriculture, they hold less than 10% of the registered land. If one adds this to the fact that women hold even less land in the largely informal but predominant customary land tenure system in the country, the sense of injustice they have endured over the years is immense.

The study demonstrates that the country's land rights model, which is predicated on the 1974 Land Ordinance, is incapable of securing equal access to land. Quite apart from that, the structure of the composition of the Board is such that those who sit on the Boards are invariably men. A major way of dealing with this injustice is to enact a revised land act with clear affirmative provisions. It will, in particular, be absolutely necessary for the new land act to draw a distinction among ownership of land, occupation and use of land.

---

[97] 2000(3)BCLR277.

The new registration system should incorporate provisions for the registration of ownership as well as occupation and use rights as distinct interest in land in the country. The proposed law should make provisions for use and occupation rights, which are predominantly in the hands of women in the rural areas, to be upgraded or converted into absolute title if they have been held for more than five years.

In doing this, Cameroon will be emulating South Africa, which in reaction to the massive land dispossessions during apartheid, enacted laws that converted tenancies held by Africans into titles. This law known in South Africa as ESTA, resulted in the vesting of substantial portions of lands in African Black Women in particular, and in Africans in general. We hereby recommend that the proposed law should contain defined detailed rules for accessing land which eliminates the barriers and obstacles against women.

Chapter Six

Mediating between Customs and Statutes in the Process of Land Registration and Enforcement of Women's Rights in Cameroon: The Role of the Administration

Florence Awasom

Abstract

This paper highlights the importance of land ownership and land disposition, and distinguishes between land possessions from land ownership. It examines the statutory stance for women to own land and how the customary law contradicts statutory law in Cameroon. Citing examples of land litigations which have disfavoured women simply because they are women, the paper argues that the presence of male traditional rulers and two notables on the Land Consultative Board tend to influence land litigations in line with traditions and customs that often disadvantage women. The paper emphasizes the fact that the gender neutrality of the Cameroon law only makes it possible for women who are financially viable to buy. But since most women are not economically empowered to buy land, they remain landless and vulnerable before customary barriers.

The paper demonstrate that statutory laws apply to all Cameroonians thereby recognizing the rights of women, widows and divorcees to own land, but nonetheless, interrogates the gender neutrality of the LCB. This is because women are considered as a lost and endangered species when it comes to land matters. Their involvement in land acquisition is timid; they are often less informed and sometimes fear traditions and cultures. The way forward, is for the land review commission consider increasing women's representative in the LCB and parliament through the quota system; encouraging traditional rulers to designate female notables to serve on the Board and; and for administrative authorities to embark on extensive rural mobilization and sensitization on land matters and especially women's rights to own land.

Introduction

Black's Law Dictionary defines land as "an immovable and indestructible three dimensional areas consisting of a portion of the earth's surface, the space above and below the surface, and everything growing on or permanently affixed to it[98]." It is obvious from this definition that land strictly construed comprises any ground soil or earth whatsoever, as meadows, pastures wood, moor mine and minerals, water, marshes furze, and heath. Land also includes all castles, houses and other buildings. There are basically two types of land: private and public land.

The ownership of land and related assets is a major prerequisite for any sustainable human growth. The right to own and dispose of land is of utmost importance both for individuals and collectivities, such as communities and including nations. In spite of this, the situation shows that in practice access to land especially to the world's poor (women) is not only limited but also insecure. According to U.N. statistics, slightly more than 1/5 of the world's population lives in extreme poverty primarily because of insecure and limited access to land. The statistics also show that of the afore-cited ratio, 75% live in rural communities (peripheral level of life) with the most vulnerable of them being women and woman headed household (single, divorced and widowed).

---

[98] **Black's Law Dictionary**, Eighth Edition (Standard Edition): Bryan A. Garner: Books

The former Commonwealth Secretary General Don MCkinnon captured the deplorable situation of women in his message to mark the 2003 International Day of the Woman when he observed that

"... Women earn 1/10 of the world's income, own less than 1/10 of the world's property and hold 1% of chief executive positions worldwide. The number of rural women living in poverty has doubled in the past 20 years and make up over 70% of the world's three billion poor who live on less than 2 dollars a day, if we want to make real headway in the fight against poverty, women must be at the heart of our strategy... Gender equality is essential for building long term sustainable and equitable development ..." It is plain from the above that increasing women's access to land and other resources is key to effect real and meaningful changes in the poverty trend in our local communities.

The primary concern of this paper is to examine the statutory provisions dealing with women's rights to acquire and own land, and to discuss how customary practices affect the proper application of property rights. The paper also reviews the mechanism for resolving land disputes with emphasis on the role played by administrative officials in resolving land conflicts. It discusses the challenges of administrative officials in their role as mediators between the demands of custom and the need for the enforcement of women's property rights in by the Land Consultative Board[99].

Women[100] and the Legal rights to own Land

The laws in Cameroon are essentially gender neutral and invariably take into consideration the need to protect equality of all Cameroonians women and men alike. Equality is enunciated in the preamble of the constitution on the basis of the principles in the

---

[99] The Land Consultative Board is the organ charged with resolving disputes pertaining to land
[100] Women used herein include; single and married women, divorcees, widows, women with children and childless women

Universal Declaration of Human Rights[101], the African Charter on Human and People's Rights and all duly ratified international conventions, including the Convention on the Elimination of all Forms of Discrimination against Women (CEDAW).

Section 16H of CEDAW stipulates that there shall be "equality between men and women with respect to ownership, acquisition, management, administration, enjoyment of property..." The preamble of the constitution of Cameroon guarantees the rights of all its citizens to own property, which *"shall mean the right guaranteed to every person by law to use, enjoy and dispose of property.* This, according to this preambular provision, means *"no person shall be deprived thereof, save for public purpose and subject to the payment of compensation under conditions determined by law."* What is more, by section 65 of this Constitution, the provisions of the preamble is justifiable since it has become an integral part of the main body of the Constitution.[102]

The courts in Cameroon have applied these statutory principles and recognized the rights of married women, divorcees and widows to own property. The case of *Debora S Wara vs. Ben Fru Wara*[103] where, in an ongoing marriage, the plaintiff sought and obtained an order of the court to cancel the sale of a house as part of property jointly acquired by both the respondent husband and herself is instructive. Similarly, in *Njim Vs. Njim née Saningong*[104] the Bamenda High Court shared the matrimonial property equally between the petitioner and the respondent wife who was given the only car on

---

[101] See Section 17 (1) of the Universal Declaration of Human Rights (UNHR), which guarantees everyone the right to own property alone, as well as in association with others

[102] It must be noted as well that in Art 45 of the constitution, provision of ratified treaties take precedence over local Cameroonian law in event of a conflict. See also Article 1 of law No. 74/1 of 6/7/74 to establish rules governing land tenure which states that "The State guarantees to all persons and corporate bodies having landed property the right to freely enjoy and dispose of such lands." This particular law does not however provide any specific advantages to women, but it consolidates the notion of private land ownership and makes it possible for any woman who can afford to acquire, own, develop, enjoy and dispose of land to so do.

[103] HCB 59/97 (Unreported)

[104] BCA/22/96

account that she had custody of minor children. This case shows the courts commitment to the principle of nondiscrimination with regards to property rights as enshrined in the constitution.[105]

Furthermore, these decisions flow from the Supreme Court decision in *CF Zamcho Florence V Chibikom Peter and 4 ors*[106] which stated inter-alia *"that any custom which subscribes to the belief or practice that a woman married or otherwise cannot inherit property is a custom which is repugnant to natural justice and good conscience and is contrary to written laws . . . ."* The above landmark case set the stage for cases like Atanga née *Nguti Rebecca Vs. The Senior Divisional Officer Ndop and 1 Or,*[107] establishing the principle that the right to landed property is quite extensive and includes the right to sue a 3rd party, including administrative officials. Thus, the applicant in the case, a married woman, successfully obtained a court ruling against the Senior Divisional Officer Ndop over a parcel of land belonging to her.

The Woman vis-à-vis Customary Land Ownership

Since under customary law, land is not clearly defined, the issue whether land includes fixtures such as air space becomes highly debatable. However, the notion of ownership of rural land is often determined by time-honoured practical ideas captured in the following questions:
-   Who inherited the land?
-   Who has occupied and developed the land (farm) over the years unperturbed?
-   Was the land bought from the original family owners in the presence of witnesses or neighbors?
-   Is it transferable without any encumbrance?
-   Does the person in occupation have a land certificate?

---

[105] See also section 77 (2) of the 1981 Civil Status Registration Ordinance that also guarantees and safeguards a widow's share of inheritance.
[106] Arrete No. 14/1 of 4/2/1993
[107] HCB/99m/97

These questions challenge the current tendency, although in general, principle individuals were not allowed to acquire land for exclusive personal use in the past. Land was communally owned with the chiefs acting as custodians of such lands. T.O. Elias, an eminent Nigerian jurist, has contended that this land right model was borne out of a desire to preserve the land for the family or community past, present and the future.[108] It is in this light that the view of the Paramount Fon of Mankon, His Majesty S.A.N. Angwafor III is to be understood. As a Fon, it is incumbent on him to preserve the heritage of the Mankon people by safeguarding and securing all land belonging to the Mankon clan.

However, the situation changed with time. After the enforcement of the 1974 law on land tenure, the rules for the management of land changed. Land now benefits the 'traditional' man at the expense of women largely due to entrenched, obnoxious and discriminatory customary practices against women across Cameroon, in spite of the country's diversified cultural groupings. The 'traditional' man has relied on the 'biblical myth' that a woman was made from a rib of a man, and the further notion that first settlement attributes all rights over land to him.

Besides, the woman is believed to be another "man's property" when she gets married. According to this view, upon marriage, the woman servers her biological link and attaches it to another family or tribe. The likelihood of transferring family heritage to a "stranger" as she is regarded in her new home is very slim. Since she cultivates land either belonging to her family, her husband or borrowed from a kinsman, she cannot cultivate perennial crops, sell nor lease the said land. Kaberry vividly captures the grass field woman's predicament thus:

"Her legal control over residential and arable land and the residual interest therein are usually in the male head of the patri-lineage and matri-

---

[108] The idea, therefore, of the alienation of land was accordingly foreign to the natives.

lineage. Women are allocated farm usufructs, access being granted to them either from their own or their husband's lineage..."

It can safely be concluded without any ambiguity that under customary rules on land tenure, women were and are not allowed to inherit or own land and landed property belonging either to their parents or husbands. Even the notion of matrilineal succession is deceptive because, under it, the boy invariably owns the land. The woman, in this case, is a mere trustee of said land. This problem has been further accentuated by early marriages, payment of bride-price, early child bearing, etc., which tend to work in favour of the son. In fact, traditional practices encourage gender inequality by promoting male stereotypes, where the woman is generally regarded as a source of wealth and subjected to male exploitations:- a chattel, sex object, baby factory, home keeper, among others. The situation is further aggravated by the fact that traditional decisions allocating land are made by the chiefs and the village traditional council on the one hand and on the other hand by clan heads and family heads who are all invariably men.[109]

Women and Land Registration

The notion of ownership of land is based not so much on whether the land in issue was acquired by inheritance, purchase or gift, but whether the land was duly registered by the purchaser. The registration of land is the legal process by which a person's legal land right is determined. The process usually commences with an application to register the land and ends when the land certificate is issued and registered in an official gazette. The main laws which

---

[109] The prevalence of these customs notwithstanding, it is a truism that customary practices, which are repugnant to natural justice, equity, good conscience and contrary to any written law (such as the Land Tenure Ordinances in Cameroon), are inapplicable and, therefore, will not prevent any woman from acquiring and developing land. This, however, is only possible where women are aware of the statutory law and have the means to seek justice in the court of law.

establish the procedure to obtain title to land in Cameroon is Decree number 76/165 of the 27th of April 1976 to establish the conditions for obtaining land certificates. It was subsequently amended and supplemented by decree number 2005/481 of the 16th of December 2005. There is also Decree number 76/166 of the 27th of April 1976 to establish the conditions of management of national lands.

These laws categorically state that the only means of obtaining title to land is by the registration of said land in the land register, which enumerates the persons and types of land that are subject to the issuance of land certificates. It also stipulates the process involved in obtaining land certificates[110]. Under the regime created by these laws, the following persons are eligible to own land in the legal sense:

- Customary communities and members there of or any person of Cameroonian nationality occupying and exploiting unregistered land pre-dating the 5th August 1974. Section 3 of Decree No. 76/126 enjoins the aforementioned persons who were in possession of the deeds listed below to automatically convert same into land certificates.

- Persons in possession of deeds of acquisition of land entered in the grund-buch.[111]

- Persons in possession of the deed of land acquired under the transcription system. This system was instituted in former East Cameroon by the French through a law of the 24th of July 1921 making it mandatory for all native citizens of the administered territory of East Cameroon to enter into a land register entitled "Livre Foncier ," all real property rights and subsequent modifications thereto.

Other types of land that fall in this category also included Land Register books or certificates of occupancy. These were proof of real property rights in former West Cameroon pursuant to the land and

---

[110] See articles 11 – 21 of decree no 76/165of 27 / 04/ 76 to establish the conditions for obtaining land certificates as subsequently amended and supplemented by Decree no 2005/481 of 16 / 12 / 05
[111] The Grundbuch was a register used by the German Colonial Master to register real property rights of the natives of Cameroon

Native Rights Ordinance of Nigeria of 1910 applicable in former West Cameroon from 1948.

- Final allocation orders for grant of state lands. This mode of acquisition is today governed by Decree number 76/166 of the 27th of April 1976 to establish the conditions of management of national lands.
- Final judgments to establish or to transfer real property rights.
- Persons in possession of deeds of acquisition of freehold lands.

Owners of Deeds

These are persons who have deeds of conveyance pursuant to direct purchase, assignments, divisions or mergers of existing registered land. It has to be noted that by section (8) (1) of the 1974 Land Tenure Ordinance, this deed of conveyance must be notarized by a public notary under pain of nullity. Under the broad terms of this legislation, the assignment of landed property entails the transfer of the initial land certificate to the purchaser or the assignee. In this case, the deed of conveyance shall be sent to the lands registrar of the administrative division, together with an application from the assignee requesting that the land be registered in his/her name.

This special procedure of getting a land certificate is the easiest and most secured way by which women can own landed property, since the land assigned or purchased is already registered and the deed of conveyance drawn up by a notary public is absolute security for the purchased land. Women who are economically viable should therefore be encouraged to purchase registered land in order to strengthen their economic activities.

Persons in Possession of Temporary Grants

A temporary grant is an informal contract entered into by an individual with the state whereby the former is allocated a portion of unoccupied and unexploited national land for development projects in line with the economic, social or cultural policies of the nation. The rules and procedure governing temporary grants are spelled out in Articles 4 to 11 of Decree number 76/166 of the 27th of April 1976 in order to establish the terms and conditions of management of national lands.

Land Litigation

In conformity with the 1974 land reforms, Decree No. 76/166 of the 27/04/76 created a Land Consultative Board and vested it with powers to sit over land disputes that touch on ownership of land and to make recommendations to the minister of lands. The Land Consultative Board, it should be emphasized, is the only statutory body entrusted with the responsibility of resolving disputes over ownership of land as well as processing land certificates (Article 12 of the 1976 Decree). The board is comprised of eight members: the divisional officer as chairman, a representative of the surveys department, a representative of the service of town planning in the case of an urban project, a representative of the ministry concerned with the project (in case of a government project), the chief of the community where the land is situated, and two leading village notables of the community where the land is situated.

This board that replaced the common law courts, which had jurisdiction on disputes over title in the past, now have the competence to examine litigations relating to ownership of land that arises before, during or after the registration of land, including:

- Disputes arising before the registration of the land: These are land litigations where two or more persons claim ownership of the land to be registered or claim possession of said land.
- Disputes arising during the registration process: These arise during the demarcation process, where an interested third party, who is apprehensive that the registration will infringe on his real property right, opposes the exercise. In such a case, the Land Consultative

Board examines the opposition on the spot and a report of the board's opinion is made.[112]

• Disputes arising after the issuance of the Land Certificate.

Disputes that arise after the insurance of land certificate may arise when:

- A person contests the land certificate issued in favour of another because he/she claims his rights have been encroached upon as a result of the registration.

- The land covered by the land certificate belongs to an applicant who was not diligent enough to oppose to the registration.[113]

- There was an error by the government services in the process of land registration. [114]

- Several land certificates are issued on the same piece of land. In this case, the first certificate that was issued prevails with the effect that the subsequently established certificates shall be declared null and void.

- The rightful owners in possession of land certificates encounter situations of squatters or trespassers on the land.[115]

The Role of the Administrative Authorities

Articles 11 to 21 of law no 76/165 of 27 /04/76 and articles 4 – 11, 12 -15(1) (2) (3) of Law no 76/166 0f 27/04/76 and other related land tenure laws makes administrative officials (Sub Divisional

---

[112] See articles 16 -20 of Decree no 76/165 of 27/04/76(supra)on the roles of the various Administrative Stake Holders in the administration of such a land dispute

[113] Here, the aggrieved part has a remedy in a civil action for damages where it is proven that the owner of the land certificate acted fraudulently. This is because the land certificate is considered unassailable, inviolate and final.

[114] Here, the minister in charge of lands has powers to order that the irregularly obtained land certificate be withdrawn and transferred to the rightful owner, provided the appeal was filed within 60 days.

[115] Law no 80/22of 14/07/1980 to repress infringement on landed property and state property gives the courts of ordinary jurisdiction competence to entertain such disputes.

Officers, Senior Divisional Officers, Regional Governors and the Minister in charge of Lands) central actors in the administration of land justice in the country.[116] Indeed, the management of litigations consequent upon the registration and ownership of land ranks amongst the main prerogatives of the civil administrator on a daily basis. The sub divisional officer by virtue of article (12) of Decree No. 76/166 of 27/04/76, who establishes the terms and conditions of national lands, is the chairman of the Land Consultative Board.

It seems plain that the sub divisional officers in their capacities as chairpersons of Land Consultative Boards plays a key role in securing land rights for women. This is more often done when, in a dispute before the Land Consultative Board, it is clearly established that the parcel of land in dispute belongs to a woman. In performing this role, the administrative officer is duty bound to ensure that all the members of the board (including the traditional representatives) objectively apply all official rules pertinent to the management of land without any bias on grounds of sex.

It is worth noting that traditional leaders (who in the North West and South West Regions of Cameroon are all men), by virtue of Decree No. 77/245 of 15/7/1977 and as modified and completed by Decree No. 82/241 of 24/6/82, are considered auxiliaries of the administration, acting as liaisons between the state and their respective communities. It is in this capacity that traditional leaders are expected to intervene (on behalf of the state) to ensure rational use of land at their respective micro levels. This administrative function is supplementary to their traditional roles as custodian of the tradition of their people and traditional custodians of communal land.

This situation raises the question whether; the law had envisaged a situation where there can be a conflict of interest within the members of the Land Consultative. These types of interest-conflicts are common especially between the Chiefs and traditional notables who are committed to their traditional beliefs and other members who may want to apply the law as it is. What is the role of the administrator as chairperson of the Board in such circumstances?

Article 15(1) of Decree No. 76/166 of 27/04/76 is instrumental since it states that the recommendation of the board shall be adopted by a simple majority of members present and shall be valid if the chief and one leading village notable participated in the proceedings. Art 15 (2) goes further to give the chairperson the right of a casting vote in the event of a tie. This, clearly, is the high point of the intermediary role of the administrative official in resolving any conflict of interest between customs and the enforcement of women's land rights during the process of land registration and litigation. There are a number of challenges to surmount in the exercise of this Herculean task.

Challenges faced by Administration Authorities

Lacuna in the land tenure law

The current land legislation does not recognize the intrinsic customary barriers with respect to women's access to land. In most traditional set ups, women are discriminated against, as they are excluded in land management even though they are the main users of land.

Section 1 of law No 74/01 of 6/7/74 presupposes an existing possessory right to the land in question in order to obtain a land certificate. This implies that after 1974, any woman who did not acquire land by purchase had to show proof of personal connection to a piece of land as a condition precedent to having a land certificate. In this situation, the obvious and most precarious consequence is that she has to revert to customary practices to ascertain occupancy or inheritance in the absence of evidence of an outright gift from a father or a husband. In this circumstance, the administration should sensitize and encourage traditional communities to ensure that women are not dealt with as right-less second class citizens because of their sex.

113

Non Recognition of Unregistered Communal Land.

The 1974 Land Tenure Ordinance has not only recognized the land certificate as the sole proof of ownership, but has also reintroduced the notion of national land involving all unregistered and unoccupied land and the notion of expropriation of "state land" for public interest. This state practice creates conflict of interest between state authorities and traditional land owners, since the latter tenaciously insist they own all ancestral land in the country that falls within what is described as communal land.

There is also the issue of multiplicity of circulars and the complexity of the land tenure laws. The country's land laws are many, complex and poorly drafted. This is further compounded by the litany of contradictions and cross references inherent these laws, which make application ineffective. The country's land model must be criticized because it is based on an undemocratic foundation. Its land legislations are mainly ordinances and presidential decrees enacted by the president and ministers and not by parliament traditionally and universally vested with powers of law making.

Cumbersome, Costly and Slow Registration Procedure constitutes a major handicap in land administration. There are too many administrative authorities involved at different levels, sometimes with functions replicating and overlapping each other. This results in unnecessary administrative bottlenecks, undue delays and at exorbitant costs to the parties.

Although statutorily the Cameroonian woman has the right to acquire and own land, in practice it remains a huge challenge due to gender inequality in decision making positions and the strong and domineering influence of customary practices in a patriarchal setting like Cameroon.

- All the ten regional governors and 58 Senior Divisional Officers in the country are men.
- Furthermore, only four out of the 380 Sub Divisional Officers are women.
- In the North West and South West regions in particular there are no female traditional leaders.

- Moreover, the designated village notables assigned to sit in the Land Consultative Boards are all men.

- These leaders and notables designated to sit on the Land Consultative Board adhere to customary practices, some of which are repugnant to basic human rights, such as: denial of inheritance rights to the daughter, abusive seizure of land where the owner is said to have committed suicide, banishment from the village, payment of royalties in Fondoms as a prerequisite to obtaining a land certificate contrary to the law in force.

- Traditional leaders appear to have a deep-rooted mistrust for women's rights. This apprehension seems to stem from a certain feeling of infallibility, particularly as they conceive their rights and powers as derived from the ancestors, which, by their peculiar view, are not subject to question.

- Most of the Fons and village notables on the board are ignorant of the legal rules regulating land. They conceive of their role in the boards as meant to ensure historical family claims to land ownership on the basis of customary rules. In the same light, most land officers, surveyors, civil administrators and ministers have no legal training and base their decisions on mainly administrative thinking, which, in some cases, is contrary to the law. Although Land Consultative Board decisions are recommendations to the minister of land, some administrative officers issue prefectural orders allocating the land to one of the disputing parties and awarding pecuniary damages, as it is now in the case in Batibo in the North West region.

- Land Consultative Board members, especially the Fons and notables, are inadequately remunerated. This invariably leads to bribery and corruption. Lack of means of transportation to disputed areas allows for exploitation of parties and the influence of decisions by those who provide transport. This is compounded by the fact that most women are illiterate and ignorant about the issues relating to land registration.

Conclusions and Recommendation

It has been demonstrated in this paper that the country's land laws, though apparently gender neutral, are in practice hostile to women and are the major obstacle for the equitable distribution of land between men and women in the region in particular and in Cameroon in general. Based on the above, it is recommended that the country's land review commission needs to go back to the drawing board and revise the laws to address the perennial question of the inequalities in land distribution between men and women in Cameroon. It is specifically recommended that:

-   A certain quota of members needs to be reserved for women in the Land Consultative Boards.

-   Gender mainstreaming strategies need to be adopted in the land management as a part of good governance, which is now prevalent in Cameroon.

-   Affirmative action will need to be taken into consideration, such as the introduction of the quota system in favor of women in key sectors of government institutions and the appointment of a certain number of female ministers in prominent ministries, as female parliamentarians, regional governors, and senior civil Service administrators.

-   Extensive sensitization of the rural population especially female farmers and female headed families will need to be carried out.

-   Education of both the formal and informal sector. Basic education should not only be free but obligatory with accompanying penal measures against those who violate such regulations.

-   More Women need to be appointed at the traditional levels.

-   Traditional leaders should designate female notables (the *Mafors*, *Yahs*, etc.) to represent their respective villages at the Land Consultative Boards (it is worthy to note that the Fondom of Batibo and Nkwen have each designated a female notable who sits on the Batibo and Nkwen Land Consultative Boards respectively.)

- The Fondoms should review the customary policy of inheritance in favor of the daughter. Daughters should not only be designated heirs in their families but they should be directly given land in their own right irrespective of their status as married or single.

- Fondoms to identify and encourage women with leadership skills to sit in traditional decision making bodies (*Ngomba*, traditional Land Dispute "Council" or "Courts"). It is obvious that female members of traditional councils will ensure that the land rights of their peers are respected and secured.

- A quota system in favor of women in need of land be introduced allowing them access to reserved state land, even if it is only for a limited period of time.

References

Akande, J (1999), Miscellany at Law and Gender Relations. Lagos: MIJ Professionals Publishes Ltd

Constitution of the Republic of Cameroon of 1972: de l'Imprimerie Nationale.

Decree No. 76/165 of 27/4/1976 to establish Conditions for Obtaining Land Certificates

Decree No. 76/166 of 27/4/1976 to establish the Terms and Conditions of Management of State Lands

Ordinance No. 74/1 of 6/7/1974 to establish Rules Governing Land Tenure

Ordinance No. 74/2 odn6/7/1974 to establish Rules Governing State Land

Ordinance No.74/3odn6/7/1974 to establish Concerning the Procedure Governing Expropriations for Public Purpose, the Terms and Conditions for Compensation

Les Editions de l'Imprimerie Nationale.

Law No. 80-22 of 14/7/1980 to Repress Infringements on Landed Property and State Lands

The International Land Coalition (2002), A Common Platform on Access to Land: The Catalyst to Reduce Rural Poverty and the Incentive for Sustainable Natural Resource Management. www.landcoalition.org

Time, C. (1999), Gender Law Report. FIDA (Cameroon) Friedrich-Ebert-Stiftung

Chapter Seven

Land Reforms in South Africa and Uganda: Practices for Enhancing the Process in Cameroon

[1]Lawrence Fombe & [2]Irene Sama-Lang

Abstract

Many African states have experienced changes in their land tenure due to colonial impact and an evolving administration. The dynamics in tenure arrangements have affected community life and caused gender inequalities in regards to access to land. Prior to colonization, this important natural resource was very accessible to the poor and the underprivileged. Land reforms in most African countries in general and Cameroon in particular have been introduced through legal frameworks which leave much to be desired due to their vagueness and lack of clarity. Implementation of Laws related to land tenure has been epitomized by administrative irregularities and misunderstandings between statutory and customary authorities.

Despite the fact that the societies from which such patriarchal laws were founded have evolved to respond to changing economic, political and some aspects of social life, issues on women's land ownership have more often been met with very stiff resistance. Women are responsible for their household livelihood, and thus access to land for food production and sustainable livelihood is crucial to them. This study, through interviews and field investigation, examines land reform approach pursued by some African countries like South Africa and Uganda to address the issues involved in ownership and access for the underprivileged groups. It aims at drawing inspiration from these countries that have made tremendous attempts to resolve their tenure problems as a prelude for similar reforms that can be adopted by policy makers, administrators and the government of Cameroon. It illustrates how good practices can positively impact women's right to land to ensure their empowerment and sustainable livelihood.

Introduction

Pre-historical customary communities in Cameroon saw land as a deity and a source of socio-cultural wellbeing.[117] Today, land is a key factor of production and development for an economy heavily reliant on agriculture like Cameroon. In the pre-colonial era of Cameroon, land ownership was clan-based and women were given rights to cultivate land allotted to them in perpetuity until death but without rights to dispose of it. This situation has not changed significantly because of the duality of conflicting laws (customary and statutory). Land reforms in Cameroon are epitomized by the revision of the Land Tenure Ordinances, which are the main laws regulating land ownership and management. The constitution remains gender neutral with regards to women land ownership rights. The application of ratified international statutes like United Nations Declaration of Human Rights (1948) and CEDAW (1981), which are gender specific and give priority of these statutes over local municipal laws, have mainly been insignificant with incidence on women's right to own land. This is so because customary laws, which are subordinate laws, are deeply entrenched in issues of land ownership, especially if it involves women who are still traditionally regarded as legal minors[118]. Courts of law are supposed to enforce statutory laws rather than to

---

117 Focus Group Workshop on Women's Land Rights in Anglophone Cameroon, March-April 2010

118 Women are regarded as legal minors according to the Fons of Ndu and Kom because they are incapable of performing the rights of pouring libation, which, in customary jurisprudence is a fundamental symbol of land ownership. Also, Section 27 (1) of the Southern Cameroons High Court law, 1955 proscribes any custom which is repugnant to natural justice, equity and good conscience or incompatible with any written law.

bow to customary laws as in the case of *Achu v. Achu*[119]. Land is still regarded as an exclusive male preserve, except when the woman has acquired a better socio-economic status or is a non-indigene[120]. In this regard, Zziwa's (1995) observations—that even if these statutes were applied they would necessitate reforms that would erode the foundation of the entrenched patriarchy and, for this reason, would make such laws ineffective–lends credence to the above assertions.

The situation in Uganda was not very different from what exist in Cameroon. The introduction of a monetary economy meant a slight shift in the pre-colonial customary laws. Land that was clan based became individualized with the colonial powers' introduction of land titling and taxes paid per head of household. Strapped for cash, these heads of households sold the lands that were now registered in their names as required by colonial laws (Tadria, 1985). With the introduction of cash crops (tea, cotton) and the subsequent cultivation of such products on lands registered in men's names, women, who provided farm labor could not lay claims over the products or the proceeds from its sale (Stamp; 1989). This signaled the beginning of the end of women's rights to land ownership in Uganda and so necessitated reforms.

South African (S.A) Land reform presents a unique situation due to its historical path from a racially dominated nation to the elimination of apartheid. The Act of 1913 prohibited Black land ownership outside the native reserves, which, at the time, constituted only 8.3% of South Africa's land area (Lahiff, 2005). According to the Native Trust and Land Act of 1936, black South Africans could not acquire land even within native reserves and land in the reserves was placed under the control of tribal chiefs. Also, a Group Areas Act of 1950 forced blacks out of land they possessed outside the homelands and compelled them to work as laborers on the white

---

119 BCA/62/86 (unreported). Customary law does not countenance the sharing of property especially landed property between husband and wife upon divorce. The wife is still regarded as the husband's property according to Justice Inglis J.
4 Interviews with the Fon of Kom and Mbengwi, February, 2009.

farms (Department of Land Affairs, 1998). This process saw about 3.5 million people removed from rural and urban areas between 1960 and 1980 and gave about 80 % of agricultural land to white South Africans. Summarily, there was thus a minority white group (<10% of the population) who owned most of the land and a dispossessed majority black group. Additionally, there was a dual system of tenure rights and land ownership by private sector and communally owned land (Lahiff, 2008). Reforms were thus relevant, given the fact that land ownership was often a source of conflict due to conquests, dispossession, forced removals and a racially–skewed distribution of land resources. Reforms have been enabled by laws established to end the landless situation of non-white communities and provisions have been made for such underprivileged persons to gain access to land.

According to Hobbs (1998), the 1963 legislation of Cameroon paved the way for the 1974 Ordinances (1, 2 & 3)[121] by reestablishing state ownership of "vacant" lands as a form of "national patrimony." The ordinances were ostensibly intended to empower the state as guardian of all land, thus ensuring rational use. Ownership was then to be recognized through titling. By this, Fisiy (1992) indicated that it led to village outsiders gaining access to land in opposition to customary traditions, which tend to allocate land to members of the resident social group. The outcome has been a massive purchase of land by elites and privileged groups (government officials and private businessmen) to the detriment of the rural underprivileged groups, the majority of whom are women, as revealed in a study by Fonjong et al (2011) in the two Anglophone Regions of Cameroon.

From the aforementioned, the crucial questions addressed in this paper are: 1) how effective have the 1974 and subsequent land reforms been able to provide equal opportunities for both the

---

121 Ordinance 74/1 of the 6th of July 1974 to establish rules governing land tenure in Cameroon. Ordinance 74/2 of the 6th of July 1974 to establish rules governing state lands in Cameroon. Ordinance 74/3 on the rules governing expropriation for public purpose and the terms and conditions of compensation.

underprivileged and women, who depend heavily on land for sustainable livelihood in Cameroon? How and to what extent have land 'reforms in countries like South Africa and Uganda successfully addressed this crucial problem of land tenure and land reforms in the midst of entrenched customary and traditional practices? And what lesson can this provide to policy makers in Cameroon?

Methodology

This study is based on field work undertaken in Cameroon, South Africa and Uganda. According to the South African Department of Land Affairs (1998), tenure reforms in South Africa have come about principally as a result of the end of apartheid and the creation of an environment for most blacks who were underprivileged that enables them gain access to land from which they were dispossessed. The underprivileged in this study have been identified to be women who are, in the majority, dependent on land and at the same time constrained by tradition to inherit family land. In Uganda, the existence of varied ethnic and cultural groups made land ownership too disparate for administration to be effective. Through an extensive literature review, South Africa and Uganda were identified as having made tremendous strides in the domain of land reforms and so constitute the take-off points for this study. Two weeks of field work in each country involved the collection of data from relevant administrative and traditional circles, which were buttressed by interviews and observations.

Documentations like the White paper in South Africa and the constitution of the various countries under study were instrumental in providing basic information on the policies and actions of the government in addressing the tenure problems. Valuable materials and information were also obtained through interviews with rural women, government officials, and university professors (University of Fort Hare in South Africa and Makerere Institute of Social Research in Uganda). Some women's groups' leaders, who have been active in bringing about land tenure reforms in Uganda and South

Africa, were also consulted to understand the various resistances put up by the civil society to enhance changes in land reforms.

The 1974 land reforms in Cameroon; status of women and the underprivileged

Land reforms in Cameroon are gender neutral, and this has given room for traditional and local administrators' practices that limit women in particular and the rural poor in general from owning land. This is evidenced by the Land Tenure Ordinance of 1974, which establishes rules governing land tenure and state lands in Cameroon. These Ordinances do not clearly define the role of women in land matters. Customary practices in most of the North and South West Regions of Cameroon consider the woman as chattel, and thus they cannot inherit family land. Even where the woman is capable of purchasing land, most often it is done in the name of the male child due to traditional influence.

The process for acquiring and owning land according to the 1974 Ordinance is very complicated, complex and cumbersome for most women who are uneducated and bound by tradition to undertake the process of purchase and certification of land. The conditions for obtaining a land certificate are poorly applied by local administrators. The land tenure ordinance, for example, does not clearly specify the financial costs to be borne by an applicant for a land certificate. The composition of the Land Consultative Board (LCB), which is the organ to study and propose files for land certificates to the government, is sex biased. This gives little room for women to have their voices heard in land matters and, consequently, leads to very few women owning land certificates compared to men. Data on land registration for selected divisions in the North West Region of Cameroon between 2000 and 2010 indicate that less than 8% of land title owners are women[122].

---

122 Regional Delegation for State Property and Land tenure, North West, 2010.

Women and land reforms in South Africa and Uganda

South Africa and Uganda have developed good practices that address their land reforms that can be emulated by Cameroon. It was observed that, in South Africa, the land issue mainly concerned the majority black population who had been deprived of land for several decades. The approach adopted in S.A in this domain is one wherein reforms have been introduced progressively (reform targets) to address specific land problems including that of discrimination in women's land rights.

The Communal Land Rights Act establishes traditional councils as the bodies that will administer communal land. The Traditional Leadership and Governance Framework Act require that 40% of the members of the traditional councils be elected and that 30% be women. The land reform policy includes a commitment to the principle of gender equity. In 1997, the Department of Land Affairs approved a 'Land Reform Gender Policy' document 'aimed at creating an enabling environment for women to access, own, control, use and manage land; as well as access credit for productive use of the land' (Department of Land Affairs 1998). These overall principles are yet to be translated into practice.

Land reforms in South Africa and Uganda are regarded in this study as 'positive efforts' not because they can be used as models, but due to the approaches and strategies that have been utilized to appease all the parties concerned (the underprivileged groups, traditional and government administrations). They constitute an on-going process in any dynamic society because of the changing environmental, political and demographic space. This is epitomized by a monetized economy, increasing urbanization, rural-urban migration that leaves behind a majority of female and youthful population who depend heavily on the land for survival, changes in land use and increasing demand for food especially from the urban population. The pace of restitution and redistribution in South Africa has been slow to the extent that the target period of 2014 might not be reached, especially for those in rural areas. In light of this, the policy of "willing buyer, willing seller" was adopted to hasten land reforms. There is much flexibility in the reform process.

Lessons of land reforms in South Africa and Uganda on women's land rights in Cameroon

In Cameroon, women's land ownership rights face obnoxious customary practices and a constitution that does not clearly address the problem. The Land Consultative Board in Cameroon, when establishing laws that clearly define the role of women in land matters, needs the input of all the parties involved.

Uganda laid a good foundation of legal and policy framework in addition to activism of the civil society at large. The role of NGOs in the gender land reform in Uganda has been invaluable. The Uganda Land Alliance (ULA), which is a consortium of local and international NGOs, is a case in point. It is the force behind the Ugandan Land Act of 1998.[123] Founded in 1995 with the aim of advocating for pro-poor land policies[124], it is made up of women's rights advocacy groups, research institutes, charity organizations and environmental groups. It was able to use research to inform all stakeholders and empower the rural women. Key provisions of the land Bill that touched on women's land rights were translated into

---

123It started off as a pressure group with the mission of ensuring that land policies and laws were reviewed to address the land rights of the poor and to protect access to land for vulnerable and disadvantaged groups and individuals.

124 Its campaigns meet these objectives focused on a number of issues. First, it attacked the principles upon which the different versions of the land bill were based and tried to demonstrate that these were detrimental to the poor. Second, it dealt with the institutional framework for controlling land and mediating the market in land. Third, it tried to demonstrate the need to protect the rights of wives and children by suggesting that land should be co-owned by the spouses and, before any land sales, the consent of wives and children must be sought. Fourth, it struggled for rights of communities to have titles. Fifth, it contributed to the lowering of the number of years from 999 to 99 during which non-citizens can hold land. Finally, it pressured the lawmakers to ensure that certificates of occupancy carried the same weight as the existing land titles.

local languages and there after the ULA held grass root sensitization and education workshop with rural women in order to mount pressure on the members of parliament to press for pro women land reforms. At the same time, they engaged members of parliaments and cabinet ministers in debates based on research findings. The ULA currently runs legal aid centers in six districts of Uganda. These legal aid centers are manned by para-legals who are not educated women from the urban centers but rather local/rural women who have received training from the ULA who educate and sensitize in the local language on land registration procedure, women's property rights during and after marriage, inheritance and succession, farming methods and conflict resolution. Though not all women of Uganda are land rights aware, from observation during field visit to Luwero district where ULA operates, the level of awareness of the women involved in discussions was very high.

The strong role played by some women's groups and the civil society in South Africa and Uganda are examples to emulate. For example, the Organisation of Women on Farms has been very outspoken about the illegal eviction of farm workers, and they demand that the implementation of current legislation must be monitored more effectively and that the socio-economic impact of evictions on vulnerable groups in rural areas of South Africa must be investigated and addressed (Mayende G, 2009)[125].

In a bid to protect the woman, the South African Human Rights Commission demanded in its submission to Parliament dated 11 November 2003 that where land is transferred to a household, the land must be registered in the woman's name as well as in the man's name (Ingunn et al, 2005). Unlike in Cameroon, Section 2 of the Ugandan Land Act 1998 vests all land in Uganda in the citizens of Uganda. In addition, section 2(a) of the Land Act 1998 recognizes

---

125 Professor Gilingwe Mayende, is lecturer at the School of Public Management and Development, University of Fort Hare, S. Africa. He was interviewed in October 2009
.

customary tenure as a system of land ownership. It has not given a time limit for the conversion of customary tenancies into freehold lands. Moreover, according to section 9 of the Ugandan Land Act 1998, anybody can apply for such conversion irrespective of the time when the person had occupied the land. This is not the case in Cameroon as persons born after 5th August 1974—the date when the land ordinances came into force—cannot apply for land certificates over national land, except if they are joined by their parents, etc. who must show that their occupation or the exploitation predates 5th August 1974. The former can only be given concessions (ordinary or long leases) over national lands. This is the position despite the fact that the preamble of the constitution provides that possession and ownership of land are sacred and inalienable rights of all Cameroonians irrespective of age, sex, religion or ethnic provenance.

In relation to women's land rights, Section 39 of the Uganda Land Act Cap 227 1998 restricts the rights of any one spouse from acting alone to dispose family land without consulting the other, thereby indirectly extending rights over family land to women. It provides that no family member or spouse shall alienate in any form land on which a family resides and from which the family derives their livelihood without prior written consent from the other spouse. The importation of parallel rights into the Land laws of Cameroon will greatly enhance the socio-economic position of poor rural women who mainly are possessors of family land in perpetuity. Section 27 of the Land Act ensures that decisions taken on customary tenure which infringes on a woman's land right are unconstitutional and so invalid, a position completely absent in Cameroon.

Since land ownership in Africa is predominantly through purchase and inheritance, Article 31(2) of the Ugandan Constitution 1995 has directed the Ugandan Parliament to take appropriate measures for the protection of spouses' rights to inherit upon the death of their partner. Upon the death of a spouse, a woman gets

15% of the deceased husband's property[126] irrespective of whether or not she has a marriage certificate. Section 65(2) and (3) of the Land Act 1998 ensures that at least one member of the land committee is a woman and that at least one member should be knowledgeable and experienced in land matters. Article 31 of the Ugandan Constitution 1995 calls for gender equity of marital parties to own and dispose of property during its subsistence and upon divorce or death. Article 32(1) of the Ugandan constitution requires the state to take affirmative action in the protection of the marginalized based on gender, which, because of history or customs, has suffered discrimination. Similar provisions that are gender sensitive are absent in the land Ordinances of Cameroon.

Existing farmers and agricultural organizations have to be accepted as credible partners in the reform process and their proposals for co-operation should be considered in good faith. Historic inequalities in land distribution are addressed in Section 25 (5, 6, and 7) of the South African Land Act. Land Reform follows a dual policy through efforts to enable the process and financial support. This is achieved through land restitution and redistribution. Restitution is an approach that intends land be returned to those who were deprived of it during apartheid or that they be compensated. Redistribution was achieved by providing land to previously disadvantaged and poor persons for residential and productive purposes, and in so-doing, meant to increase black ownership of land in S.A. There is also a Communal Land Act that protects the tenure rights of people who live on communal or tribal land. In the arrangement, customary land remains under the control of traditional rulers who have lost such rights in the past. According to South African customary law on inheritance, only male children can inherit land which also still applies to 'black African' people living not only

---

126 This has been challenged by FIDA Uganda and other women advocacy groups as being too insignificant. In this regard, the Constitutional court of Uganda declared this as being unconstitutional (Kasanda Sarah Kahiha FIDA Uganda interviewed on 5th November 2009). It is however still awaiting parliamentary confirmation.

in the former reserves, but also in urban areas. But when land is transferred to a household, the land is registered in the woman's name as well as in the man's name (Ingunn et al, 2005). This would illustrate a firm commitment to addressing the endemic situation of the Cameroon woman, if incorporated in the country's constitution.

Conclusion

The context within which land reform programs are implemented involves the necessity that land reform must contribute to real socio-economic transformation. The debate on land reforms in South Africa and Uganda is still an ongoing process, as many institutions, political parties and NGOs in addition to the government continue to look for better and more pragmatic paradigms to address the issues of land laborers/dwellers, ethnicity, land quality and location as well as the plight of the women in a bid to relieve rural poverty and to ensure sustainable livelihood. The beneficiaries of the land reform program are defined primarily in terms of race as in S.A. or in terms of gender as in Uganda. These governments, however, recognize that past policies have led to skewed gender relations in terms of access to productive resources. The right to equality between men and women is stated in the Constitutions of these countries, but in Cameroon, the land reform policy should include a commitment to the principle of gender equity. The government should be committed to ensuring that gender issues are considered in all its policies and programs, especially as it has signed various international conventions and declarations aimed at advancing the interests of women.

Legal support and communication is an important issue in land reform for the Cameroonian woman. The majority of women are ignorant of the process of land registration that can give them permanent control over land. They do not know where to get help, and are thus marginalized in legal processes. This is linked to legal support especially where legalized marriages give the woman greater opportunities to have control and be able to manage family land in case of the loss of her husband. If well sensitized, this can be a niche for the woman to stand firmly against some of the obnoxious traditional practices that keep her away from exercising her marital role.

Recommendations

Land reform should straddle socio-economic and technological developments within the society. Failure by the constitution of Cameroon to adequately address the gender issue of land ownership has resulted in increasing marginalisation of women and thereby adversely affected livelihood in most communities. It is necessary for policy makers to seriously address this problem by putting in place structures and well-defined laws that can cater for the interests of the various social classes of the society. Specifically, the following recommendations can constitute important inroads for land reforms in Cameroon as epitomised by the good practices of South Africa and Uganda.

• The Cameroon government just like in S. Africa and Uganda, should create an enabling environment through forums not only with the legislature, but within rural areas, making use of traditional authorities, women group leaders and NGOs to propose better approaches to embrace the issues related to access and ownership of land and to give equal opportunities especially for those groups that heavily rely on land for their livelihood.

• Education of women on the dynamics of land and titling is indispensable. Growing population and mounting pressure on land has meant greater speculation and incorporation of rural land into more urban functions. The example in S.A. wherein the homelands could no longer contain an exploding population is glaring. Ownership of land can be a key to a more sustainable livelihood and a peaceful environment for development. Women can substantially contribute to development if empowered through land ownership and well educated.

• Reforms should be progressively implemented. There is need for flexibility to achieve defined landmarks that meet the needs and aspirations of all classes of the society. This can give room for better assessment and modifications of poorly adopted and poorly implemented policies.

References

Cousins, B & Claassens, A. (2004), Communal land rights and democracy in post-apartheid South Africa. Paper presented at the conference, *The politics of socio-economic rights in South Africa: Ten years after apartheid,* University of Oslo.

Constitution of Cameroon 1996.

Cross, C & Hornby, D. (2002), Opportunities and obstacles to women's land access in South Africa. A research report for Promoting Women's Access to Land Programme, February 2002. www.nlc.co.za/pubs2003/womenlandaccess/wlatoc.htm

Department of Land Affairs, (1998), White Paper on South African Land Policy.

Department of Land Affairs. (1991), White Paper on Land Reform. [Online]. Available:

http://land.pwv.gov.za/white%20paper/whitefir.htm   (Accessed, October 2009).

Fisiy, C. F. (1992), *Power and privilege in the administration of law: land law reforms and social differentiation in Cameroon,* Leiden, The Netherlands, African Studies Center.

Fonjong, L. Sama-Lang , I. and Fombe L. (2011), Report on *the Impact of Land Tenure Practices on Women's Rights to Land in Anglophone Cameroon and Implications on Sustainable Development.* IDRC Project No 105467. University of Buea IDRC, Canada.

Hobbs, M. (1998), Country profiles of land tenure; Africa, 1996 in Land tenure centre.Accessed from http://pdf.wri.org/ref/elbow_98_synthesis.pdf November, 2011.

Ingunn Ikdahl; A. Hellum; R. Kaarhus; Tor A. Benjaminsen & P. Kameri-Mbote. (2005). Studies in Women's Law No. 57, *Institute of Women's Law*, Revised version of Noragric Report No. 26, June 2005, Norwegian University of Life Sciences, Oslo.

Lahiff, E. (2005), "Debating land reform, natural resources and poverty." PLAAS Policy Brief, No. 17.

Lahiff, E. (2008), Land Reform in South Africa: A Status Report, 2008, PLAAS, School of Government, UWC, Cape Town.

Nyangabyaki- Bazaara. (2000), 'Civil society and the struggle for land rights for marginalized groups: The contribution of the Uganda Land Alliance to the Land Act 1998'; *Civil Society and Governance Programme IDS* available at: http://www.ids.ac.uk/ids/civsoc/final/ uganda/Uga3.doc

Stamp, P. (1989), Technology, Gender and Power in Africa, Technical Study 63 E.

Tadria, K.M., (1985), Changing Economic and Gender Patterns Among the Peasants of Ndejje and Sseguku in Uganda. Doctoral Dissertation, University of Minnesota, USA in Zziwa, A. J, (1995), Research Paper 16 on Gender Perspective on Land Ownership and Inheritance in Uganda, MISR and University of Wisconsin-Madison, USA.

The UN Convention on the Elimination of All Forms of Discrimination against Women (CEDAW). Adopted 18 December 1979, entered into force 3 September 1981, South Africa: Initial report submitted in 1998 (CEDAW/C/ZAF/1) Initial report examined by the Committee at the 19 session (1998), concluding observations and comments published in A/53/38/Rev.1 (1998), Part 2 (session 19) paras 100-137.

Zziwa, A. J. (1995), Research Paper 16 on Gender Perspective on Land Ownership and Inheritance in Uganda, MISR and University of Wisconsin-Madison, USA.

Chapter Eight

Discrimination in Women's Property and Inheritance Rights in Cameroon: The Role of Human Rights NGOs in Promoting Gender Sensitive Land Reforms

Harmony Bobga

Abstract

The main land legislation regulating land tenure in Cameroon is over 36 years old and, although it has been undergoing some amendments, it is still far from complying with current realities. Even though every Cameroonian citizen has rights to land ownership as per the laws, this is not the case in practice where growing inequalities exist. Women constitute the group mostly discriminated against. This discrimination can be blamed on the socio-political and legal environment which includes both modern and customary laws. Inheritance is the predominant mode of accession to land and either through testate or intestate succession. But the mosaic of customary communities with different customs and traditions place women in the disadvantaged position. This paper describes the situation of these women and observes that it is important to go beyond customs and traditions as well as beyond post-independence legislations to analyse and enhance women's land rights in Cameroon. It holds that NGOs can play an important role in redressing the situation of women. While attempting to define NGOs, the paper discusses the nature of their participation in the land reform process and who should participate. It concludes that community education, affirmative litigation, research and publication constitute some of the activities these NGOs can undertake as part of their participation.

Introduction

The challenges of translating human rights into concrete gains have, in the last decade, been laid bare by the elusiveness of most of the millennium development goals that the world, under the auspices of the United Nations Organization, set for itself. The most recent indicators of this failure of the world's socio-economic system have emerged as economic/financial melt-downs in the United States of America and the European Union. Enormous efforts are still being deployed to diagnose the problems within the bell jar of performance restricted to failed economic theories and incorrect figures of financial reliability projections.

One foundational area of diagnosis which seems to have been deliberately ignored is that of the inequity in the distribution of the wealth of the world not only spatially but, more importantly, across gender. The inequality between the rich and the poor has been presented persistently as a ration between the rich industrial west (especially) and the "so-called" third world or poor nations. Even apparent figures indicating this disparity 'are pricks that do not yet get to the bone.' The real question is why the inequalities between male and female in the world over, or simply what is the share of the world's wealth that each of these gender groups holds? But what access to this wealth existed, exists, and will be available to each of these two groups in future? Is there not an urgent need to reconfigure the access to wealth and therefore wellbeing consequent upon which there could be assurance of a gender balanced and sustainable human development?

It will be too ambitious to embrace these questions at a global level all at once. The recently concluded IDRC-University of Buea Women's Land Rights Project (2008-2011), helped to profile and raise awareness on women's access to land as a means of empowerment. Women's empowerment widens their access to wealth through land ownership and thus assures sustainable and greater human development in the two "Anglophone" Regions of Cameroon. The IDRC-University of Buea project offers a unique window for making attempts at answering important development questions, starting with women's property and inheritance rights as a specific pathway into women's ownership of land, which incidentally, accounts for the soul of wealth anywhere in the world.

The geographic area attributed to "Anglophone Cameroon" will however not be taken in isolation. Being a "lesser solution" in the Cameroon Republic setting, with the stronger solution being in the "Francophone Cameroon, there will be occasional insights into the Anglophone/Francophone differences in gender sensitivities to rights to property [land] and acquisition of that right through inheritance. By cracking through the big questions and beginning first with inquiring into the foundational kernel questions, this paper will examine the issues outlined in the course of the discussion

Research Problem

A key principle and rule enshrined in the Constitution of Cameroon is equality before the law. Regrettably, in the area of women's property rights and the means of acceding to those rights and in particular through inheritance, it is no understatement to assert that the constitutional "guaranty" is a classic case of constitutional duplicity, given what it obtains in practice. The consequences of this situation singularly and collectively undermine both women's civil and political rights and their economic social and cultural rights, the ultimate effect of which is a compromise of women's right to human development

The select sets of issues that arise from looking through the window referred to above into the problematic realm of women's property and inheritance rights and the challenges to turning the situation around, raise a number of pertinent questions, but which, for the purpose of this paper, are restricted to the following:

1. Do women's property rights have a secure legal conception in Cameroon?

2. Do land registration and land and property inheritance rights as practiced today provide equal space for men and women?

3. To what extent do Non-governmental Organizations and women's rights Groups fully comprehend and can contribute to/foster land reforms to improve women's property and land inheritance rights in Cameroon? And how effective have their efforts been in unblocking the situation of landless women in the country? Finally,

4. Can affirmative action in land reforms translate into a productive and sustainable culture of women's land rights with ultimate benefits for the Cameroon nation?

Scope of the Study

While this research will address the identified problem over women's property and inheritance rights in Cameroon generally, the focus of the inquiry will be on the common law jurisdiction(s) operative within the dominantly civil law context of Cameroon. In the process, however, occasional comparison will be made not only between the Common Law and Civil Law, but also between but also between the "modern" law and the mosaic of customary laws of Cameroon, derived from the customs and traditions of the autochthonous constituent of Cameroonian communities.

Methodology

There is a paucity of published literature on women's property [land] rights and access thereto, particularly through inheritance in Cameroon. The few works that exist do not even address the specific problem of women's rights to accede to property ownership through inheritance, for that matter.

The methodology adopted in the survey of this research involves a theoretical re-conceptualization of women's property rights and their rights to accede to property ownership through inheritance, by drawing heavily from general principles of land ownership as read with the provisions of the Convention for the Elimination of Discrimination against Women.

Some decided cases touching and concerning issues related to women's economic, social and cultural rights have been reviewed to demonstrate the inadequacy of security of women's property rights in Cameroon. This, of course, is being accompanied by an identification and evaluation of the role of non-governmental Organizations and Groups that have done work in the direction of improving women's access to land, especially through inheritance in Cameroon. Each of the identified issues for discussion/analysis leads to the conclusions of "what is." Thereupon, proposals for review of substantive laws and procedures for an affirmative reform of women's land rights shall be made along with proposals for the role that NGOs/Groups would be required to play in translating the reforms, once secured, into a sustainable culture of realizable women's land rights in Cameroon.

The security of the concept of women's property [land] rights within the Cameroon legal system(s)

In law, the meaning that is attached to something is critical to understanding and dealing in that thing in a very specific manner in every legal system. The conception of land in Cameroon is no exception to this truth. Furthermore, the underlying and surrounding cultural practices are undeniably affective to the concept of land. In Cameroon, there exists a mosaic of legal systems competing with one another, "breathing" meaning into legal concepts. In the process, those concepts translate into practical realities. As far as property [land] ownership is concerned in Cameroon nationally, the only statutorily recognized concept of "landed property[127]" is "registered

---

[127] Land, as a matter of fact, is described in its physical form –An immovable and indestructible three-dimensional area consisting of a portion of the earth's surface, the space above and below the surface, everything growing on or permanently affixed to it. 2. Its ownership relates to the fact of a person having such degree of

land[128]." This is provided for in Decree 76-165 of 27th April 1976 to establish the conditions for obtaining land certificates, which reads thus:

Article 1
(1) "The land certificate shall be the official certification of real property rights."
(2) Subject to the provisions of Articles 2(3) and 24 of this Decree, land certificates shall be unassailable, inviolable, and final. The same shall apply to documents certifying other real property rights.
(3) When registered in a special register called the Land Register, a real property right shall be deemed registered and may be opposed to third parties.

From the above gender-neutral legislative representation of the legal meaning and nature of real property right(s) under Cameroon law, it is hard to read from the face of the legislative provision(s) any problem that women may have or could raise with respect to their access to land ownership. However, when the same meaning is put in the context of the history and wider "operative legal cultures" of Cameroon, the practical reality from the perspective of women is that their access to land ownership is constricted. Women's rights to affirmative action[129] as a strategy for balancing their access to rights in general and real property rights in particular with that of men,

---

control over it that is superior to that all other persons, i.e. an estate or interest in real property.
[128] Registration is the process of securing administrative recognition of the fact of superior control over land. Under Cameroon legislation the theory is that the land registration process gives birth to the fact of, and legal recognition of ownership of land.
[129] This is the mechanism of given some special treatment or advantage to women as a means of balancing up their situation from historical discrimination from men so that a process is set in motion for translating professed gender equality in constitutions into reality.

becomes evident and urgent if there is an objective to let them benefit from the constitutional right of equality before the law[130].

Another factor crucial to understanding the concept of land ownership, which is distorted by the current mechanical interpretation of the legislative provision on land ownership, is that the "juridico-metaphysical" process of creating land ownership. This process is vulnerable to being overstretched such that there emerges an unavoidable risk of the narrow construction blinding the physical and practical reality of how land ownership arises.

A review of the process of land registration reveals that the "person" who applies for and obtains administrative recognition that she or he owns a particular parcel of land, has, as a precondition, an unchallenged inter-relationship to the land [the object], and that that person's claim is superior to the claim(s) of any other person(s)[131]. From this perspective, it becomes clearer that the pre-registration inter-relationship between the person and the parcel of land bears "a quantum of interests/rights," which the land registration process simply delivers into legality, and which is not to be ignored. This position is the more pertinent, because the point is that most women, especially rural women, are physically in possession of land they occupy and cultivate but which, by the legislative provision regarding land ownership, they "do not own" and may never own on account of the combination of the "cultural mythologies and practices ," complicated by gender-biased procedures for land registration.

It follows from the foregoing that if the statutory definition of land is not reviewed and up-scaled to include in the phrase "ownership of land" to the rights that immediately underlie or precede registration of land, there is a risk of perpetuating a concept of land ownership that impedes women's access to land ownership.

---

[130] Cameroon Constitution (Law No. 96/6 of 18th January 1996 – paragraph 4 page 4) states [All persons shall have equal rights and obligations...]
[131] Nyama, J.Me (2001). Regime Foncier et Domanialite Publique Au Cameroun, Presses de L'UCAC.

While the redefinition of land ownership on the Cameroon statute books is awaited, the accession to ownership of land through registration, inheritance, and purchase under the present regime still poses grave problems to women as opposed to their male counterparts. We shall now examine these three paths of accession to land ownership.

Gender and Accessibility to Land Ownership

The mere fact of being born a female is an obstacle to ownership of property. What accounts for this discrimination is deeply entrenched in the perception of women by society. The unsupportable attitudes towards women in this regard are wrongly justified from the historical foundation of society and especially its systems for regulating the inter-relationships of members of the society, i.e. the laws. Women's access to ownership of land is constricted on the basis of gender differentiation and discrimination in the following three areas: land registration, inheritance of land, and acquisition of land by purchase.

Women's Access to Land through Land Registration

Unlike it is understood and applied in other national jurisdictions, land registration in Cameroon represents a metaphysical process by which ownership of land is created. This is the import of Article 1(1), (2), and (3) of Decree No. 76-165 of 27th April 1976 that establishes the conditions for obtaining land certificates, as amended by Decree No. 2005/481 of 16th December 1976 which reads:

1. "The Land Certificate shall be the official certificate of real property rights;
2. Subject to the provisions of Articles 2(3) and 24 of this Decree, land certificates shall be unassailable, inviolable, and final. The same shall apply to documents certifying other real property rights.

3. When recorded in a special register called a Land Register, a real property right shall be deemed registered and may be opposed to third parties.

It is evident from the phraseology of the subsections quoted above that none of the subsections are intended by the legislator to be independent of the others. It follows that the allusion to "official certification" in sub-section (1) does not refer to a certification process simplifier. This if treated in isolation, would create room to look back at the relevance and implications of the quantum of interest in the parcel of land prior to the registration. The registration of that parcel of land with inscription in the land register will infer that the "certification process" turns an unregistered interest into something now legal, as opposed to the process of registration being the "magic" process by which the right in the parcel of land in question is created out of nothing!

This idea that legal land right over a specific parcel of land is a process of creation of something from nothing is borne graphically from the character of "unassailability ," "inviolability ," and finality. Curiously, Article 1(3) emphasizes the magic process of entry into, or registration in a special register which is then deemed registered and upon such registration becomes automatically opposable to third parties.

Article 2 as borne out of the 2005 amendment by Decree No. 2005/481 of 16th December 2005, produces in the letter of its sub-sections contradictory theories. However in their spirits, they reinforce the metaphysical nature of the process of "land registration" as representing the unique point of conception and delivery of the only feasible land ownership right. Under Articles 9(a) and (b) and 10 of the Decree, the "persons" who are eligible to apply i.e. acquire legal title by obtainment of land certificate over parcels of land include as in Article 9.

(a) Customary communities, members thereof, or any other person of Cameroonian nationality on condition that the occupancy or the exploitation predates 5th August 1974, date of publication of

Ordinance No. 74-1 of 6th July 1974 to establish rules and regulations governing land tenure;

(b) Persons who have forfeited their rights as a result of the application of Articles 4, 5, and 6 of the above mentioned Ordinance.

Article 10 of the Decree further puts a negative qualification on the foregoing conditions of eligibility for applying for a land certificate in the following terms: "The Trustees of an inheritance may not obtain land certificates for their properties in their own names."

It is noticeable from the opening phrase of Article 9(a) — "customary communities, member's thereof…"—that the Cameroonian legislator places great emphasis on customary community with the attendant implication that the customs and traditions of such communities play a critical role in the acquisition of land certificates. This position is further strengthened by the composition of land consultative Boards which include the traditional authority and two of his notables who generally are males and, as such, exclude female representation. Invariably, the discriminatory character of customs and traditions that weigh heavily against women slips here, and signals a constriction of women's access to land ownership through registration.

Besides the traditional authorities and their notables, it is obvious that with the male dominance in the institutional structures through which Land certificates are processed, women are cut out as strangers to the process, rendering the process highly vulnerable to gender insensitivity and to the disadvantage of women.

The problem of discrimination against women in the registration process as a means of accession to real property rights under Cameroon law is not restricted to the foregoing situation when it goes down without a hitch. However, there are even more critical hurdles when disputes arise in the registration process. First, there is the question of cost which, on account of women's low access to credit. Second, there is also a very long, but slow, technical, and complicated procedure for land disputes resolution and adjudication, which readily deter most women. This is because it is more likely than not, to turn into a self-inflicted persecution by the simply exercise of the choice to engaged the disputes process.

It is also noteworthy that from the population pyramid of Cameroon, the majority of women today could not have been of such age that qualified them to be "occupiers" or "exploiters" of parcels of lands within specific customary communities prior to the 5th day of August 1974 to be eligible to apply for registration of such lands. Even those women who were farming on the lands as of that cutoff date, customs and tradition in most customary communities considered them as "property" that was thus considered in turn to be incapable of "owning property"! Even though this view that women are properties has been abrogated by both statute and precedent, its spirit lingers on to date and rules women's property rights from its grave. It is also this dead but alive principle which runs against the current of natural justice equity and good conscience, as it violates the very dignity of women as human beings, that lay at the base of yet another avenue by which access to land ownership by women is constricted, as examined hereunder.

Women's Access to Land through Inheritance.

To inherit means to receive property from a previous owner upon that owner's death. Land is one of the most commonly inherited categories of property in developing societies and thus is generally highly regulated, whether it is under "customary ," or "modern" laws. In the histories of both customary and modern laws, gender imbalances against women as respects the rights and practices of inheritance abound.

In Cameroon, where modern laws which bear a relatively greater gender balance in inheritance laws and practices are as a matter of reality merely a thin film floating over a mosaic of well entrenched and highly active customs and traditions that regulate devolution of property upon the death of its deceased owner. Incidentally these customs and traditions that are somewhat crystallized in the psyche

145

of the native African Cameroonian even when he or she is clothed in western clothing and education are for the most part gravely discriminatory against the female gender.

Given that historically the land owners in customary communities that constitute Cameroon were from origin males who by the customary inheritance practices perpetuate male dominance through inheritance customary rules and practices, it is obvious that female inheritance is an emergent concept. Even in customary communities wherein "matrilineal succession is practice, women like their wombs are treated merely as conduits for transmission and really do not hold substantive benefit of the devolution of property because under the said system, the person of the women only facilitates passage to her son, yet another male, of her late brother's property [land].

There are many instances where the questions of gender biases have reared their ugly heads in the course of adjudicating over devolution of property to female successors-in-title. Some of such cases will be briefly summarized hereunder and commented upon to demonstrate the prevalence of the problem of narrow access open to women to accede to property [including land] ownership from deceased persons.

Women's Access to Land through Purchase

Another possible means by which a woman may acquire and effectively own property is through purchase. From wage-earnings and returns from trading or other profitable services deliveries, thanks to more women having obtained empowerment for them through education, a reasonable crop of women have or are capable of accumulating wealth enough to actually purchase and own land.

It has been argued that the "poor" in developing countries do actually save from their dire situation more than three times the total that the "developed" countries send to those poor countries as "Aid"! A cursory look at the gender representation in, for example the Credit Union Movement especially in the North West and South West Regions of Cameroon bears indicators that more women

146

particularly from the lower rung of our society contribute to the staggering amounts that the Credit Unions collect as savings from the "poor." It follows that collectively the women folk have more money that is saved than their men folks. The issue now is how easily do these women use this financial power?

The answer is rarely and when they do it is more often than not for "servicing" their men! Married women buy land and build houses for their male relations. This is not natural generosity. It is rather predicated upon the pervading and persisting cultural clichés that ownership of land is reserved for men. When women actually seek to purchase and own land themselves, more often than not they are seen as acting out of the ordinary. Quite often they receive cynical compliments like "...that woman is really a man."

Practically, and this is quite pertinent, vendors of land rarely would sell to women forcing women to acquire landed property by purchase through male relatives or friends with the attendant risk of losing the property should the male land purchase medium decide to breach the trust between him and the actual buyer who is a woman. When it is a married woman who seeks to acquire property by purchase, the convenient but ultimately discomforting argument is that the couple constitutes a unit and it is not necessary for the woman to own her own property as if the marital union is no longer a going concern in which the man is not simply the "protector" of the person of the woman but of her proprietary interests especially when it comes to real property[132]. The case of single women is even more precarious given that the stigma of being single even renders them vulnerable to various kinds of abuses, lending itself to ready acceptance of the "protection" of a man in a bid to secure their property rights.

From the foregoing discussions, it is not deniable that women's access to land ownership in Cameroon generally and in the North West and South West Regions in particular, gender biases do account

---

[132] Arnaud, A.J. and Kingdom, E. (1990). Women's Rights and the Rights of Man. Enlightenment, Rights and Revolution Series; Aberdeen, University Press

for a constricted access to land ownership for the Cameroonian woman. It is also evident that this is not a problem that seems to lend itself for solution or meaningful amelioration from state institutions exclusively. Civil society organizations like non-governmental organizations do seem to have an important and critical role to play in turning the ugly situation around for the ultimate good of society without any gender differentiation, in the short and medium terms for specific cases and in the long term, through mobilization sensitization and campaigning for gender-balanced land reforms.

It is therefore now proposed to examine what the roles that NGOs have played and can play further in providing solutions to gender discrimination in the area of land ownership. This exercise, which shall be based on NGO and partners experiences in the two focal regions constitute our next focus.

Women's NGOs and Gender-balanced Land Reforms

This paper in the preceding section diagnosed the problematic of women's inheritance and land rights. The following section focus principally on formulating strategies to overcome the problem as diagnosed. In so doing, it attempt a review on the approaches so far been used, the actors involved and the successes and failures so far have been recorded. It is believed that using the SWOT analysis, a platform for using the past to understand the present in order to better chart the path into the future for better results would be set.

Past Strategies of Improving the Security of Women's Inheritance and Property Rights

In pre-colonial times the idea of exclusion of women from inheritance and land rights was at its highest water mark. This is because it was crystallized in the psyche of not just the individuals but the customary communities that were through colonialism mapped into "one" country, that women constituted heritable property themselves. It could thus never be contemplated that "property could in the wildest of imaginations could inherit or own property."

Through the judicial systems that the colonialist put in place in the newly created territories seeds of elimination of the indignities of considering women as heritable property began to be sown. These seeds were just in line with other obnoxious customs and traditions that have been the sources of law in the pre-colonial period. In Southern Cameroons[133] for example, the limits of customary laws were set as follows:

Upon accessions to independence, the two Cameroons made allusions in the preambles of their Constitutions to respect for human rights which inherently included women's rights. Women rights at best could be considered peripherally or indicative because they were not yet constitutional provisions that could effectively be invoked and enforced like other substantive parts of those constitutions. The so-called unification that progressively ushered in a Federal constitution followed by a unitary constitution did not remedy the situation. It was only in the 1996, that the provisions in the preamble of the Constitution, which included human rights provisions, were upgraded to status of substantive enforceable parts of the constitution, through its Article 65[134]. Furthermore, Article 45[135] of the same 1996 Constitution raised the normative value of human rights conventions adopted in the preamble to the pinnacle of the hierarchy of legal norms in Cameroon, through state obligation under international law to respect of international agreements.

The constitutional foundations created in 1996 for better security of women's inheritance and land rights, have not in themselves changed much for women for two reasons: In the first place, there is

---

[133] Southern Cameroons High Court Law, 1955

[134] "The Preamble shall be part and parcel of this constitution." This may be referred to as the human rights entrenchment provision.

[135] "Duly approved or ratified treaties and international agreements shall, following their publication, override national laws, provided the other party implements the said treaty or agreement."

yet to be put in place the human rights enforcement rules of procedure. Secondly, the direct laws on inheritance and property rights have not been amended to conform with the constitutional provisions on human rights to permit full benefit to be taken thereof. The writing of Last Wills and Testaments is yet to become fashionable, and thus devolution of a deceased's property is largely still ruled by customs and tradition as personal law of the deceased.

Above the foregoing impediments, there has been an equally serious of ignorance which puts to question from point of equity, the maxim that "ignorance of the law is not a defense" when applied to the question of inheritance and land rights of the woman. Awareness creation has thus been a major necessity in the activities geared towards enhancing women's inheritance and land rights. The mapping of the evolutionary legal environment of the security of women's inheritance and land rights thus call for an inquiry on the who?, what?, how?, and when?, "Women's NGOs have fared with working for greater security of women's rights in these tow thorny areas.

The Who?

One of the big issues in combating discrimination against women is that of identification of "the enemy." Obviously "men" and their regroupings are generally considered the number one enemy of women's problems arising from gender-based discrimination such as those that impede women's inheritance rights and access to land. This explains why with the opening of "civil and political space" in Cameroon following the launching of the first post-1990 opposition political party, there followed a surge-like emergence of NGOs. The scene was dominated by men and slowly followed by Women's NGOs which focused exclusively on women's rights issues. There is however, no denying the fact that while "men" are part of women's problems they are also an integral part of the solution to those problems. It follows therefore that those that have so far thought of women's NGOs as the only vehicles that are appropriate for enhancing women's rights are not entirely right. Half the solution lies in mobilizing, sensitizing and conscientizing men towards acknowledgement acceptance and accommodation of women as humans equally entitled to respect of the inherent dignity of the human person and the rights that flow there from.

The past perception that only women can do it for women needs rethinking so that from a synergic strategic angle, men could profitably be fully integrated into the projects for uplifting women's rights in general and those relating to inheritance and access to land, in particular. In fact, the "Who" in the fight for women's rights in this case so urgently need a positive and inclusive reconfiguration.

The What?

The fostering of women's inheritance and land rights, simple as it may appear and sound, requires discerning in order that the substance of the goal may be properly understood and mastered to avoid shooting off tangent. It is a lot more than marketing the idea of women's "inheritance rights," and "land rights." It involves mobilization and sensitization of much more than just the affected subjects. It requires, as a sustaining accompaniment, the conscientization of the real and perceived blockers of access to those rights. Focus on institutions and processes that impact on access to enjoyment of the rights in issue is also necessary. Such focus unavoidably will include traditional institutions, modern state structures, civil society organizations/NGOs, and even individual actors.

The How?

It is a truism that governments are hardly whistle blowers against themselves. Civil society organizations/NGOs take center stage in whistle blowing in matters where the objective is to push governments to act. The problematic of women's inheritance and land rights in Cameroon and the need for legislative reform in the area is a matter best handled by Civil Society Organizations/NGOs. The suitability of Civil Society Organization/NGOs is vulnerable to the limited capacities of individual member organizations of the civil Society/NGO communities. The attainability of the set objectives therefore require a combination of macro and micro strategies in responding to the needs of formulating and executing projects geared towards fostering reforms in the areas of women's inheritance and land rights.

Most, if not virtually all Civil Society Organizations/NGOs in Cameroon are not only financially dependent on foreign financing, but lack expertise for optimal performances on the projects they set themselves for. There exist therefore institutional and individual personnel incapacities which constitute serious draw-back factors in performance. The matter is even compounded by foreign financing that comes with strings. Most foreign funding have political-economic strings, which when carefully studied are hardly accidental occurrences. Indeed, they constitute deliberate hidden agendas for undermining human development in less developed countries like Cameroon.

It follows that if individual NGOs were to embark on the project of fostering women's inheritance and land rights especially in the direction of legislative reform, going it in dispersed ranks would be most unhelpful for their individual energies and capacities would hardly jump start them sufficiently. A collective approach amongst the NGOs from baseline studies through monitoring and evaluation is more likely to produce greater impact. This could be married with distribution of tasks amongst NGOs or groups thereof according to the various capacities (personnel and institutional), geographic locations and past experiences. Common methodologies in order to ensure similarities in outcomes could include participatory grassroots appraisals, roundtable discussions with major local stakeholders through the political structures such as village community organizations, Sub-Divisional, Divisional, Regional and National conferences on same themes from bottom to top. The use of the media in an agreed uniform delivery manner from package to method is also worthy.

The judiciary could also be lobbied through advocates handling cases through which legislative change could be promoted, to make pronouncements that foster acceptability of positive and affirmative change in the law and practice of women's inheritance and land rights. The private Bar in collaboration with NGOs could also take up a joint project of widening access to justice for women in the area of inheritance and land rights.

Curriculum development is equally another effective long term tool. From basic education through secondary up to tertiary education levels , mainstreaming women's rights would set in motion a long term change in attitudes and ultimately cultures that are anti-women and thereby ensure the emergence of inclusivity in favour of women in enjoyment of human rights in general and inheritance and land rights in particular.

Most parents are simply trapped in the customs and traditions that are anti-women's inheritance and land rights. NGOs may make a great difference by promoting the writing of wills by parents through which the door could be shut on the discriminations against women in issue.

The above methods could be used by NGOs within a networking framework or consortium as has been tested successfully before in Cameroon[136] and elsewhere[137]. This wise the NGOs can more easily constitute a force sufficient to provide legislative lobbying fire on government to consider legislative change in the area of women's inheritance and land rights. This may not stop simply at asking but

---

[136] The Canadian Pro-Democracy Project conceived and executed in Cameroon in the '90s actually brought several NGOs together who jointly carried out the baseline studies and after profiling of the participating NGOs, tasks were distributed through presentation and selection of projects for funding in thematic and geographic areas on a common agenda for improving the human rights and democracy situation in Cameroon.

[137] In South Africa and American sponsored human rights and democracy project equally created a consortium of NGOs that executed a common project as a collaborative endeavor amongst them.

the NGOs could engage experts to draft the bill and open debate on it in the media. This is one way to demonstrate the urgent need for change that would bring conformity of local/national legislation with international conventions on human rights under which Cameroon has obligations.

Research and publication is another tool with which deeper insights into the problem of women's inheritance and land rights can be obtained. It is suggested that undergraduate and graduate students alike should be encouraged especially in the departments of law and Women and gender studies to undertake grassroots research for either their term papers or final year projects. Such works will build a useful store of knowledge from which best practices could be filtered and blended with modern human rights concepts and by that a synergic marriage of local realities and modernities could give birth to a sustainable and progressive corpus juris on women's inheritance and land rights. The materials will also provide basis for further qualitative research works at the tertiary levels.

"The when?"

The time is now because IDRC/UB Women's Land Right project has set the project in orbit and the momentum it has gathered ought not to be allowed to die out. Cameroon is also into electoral effervescence[138] which allows civil society to secure commitments from politicians and elective public office aspirants to reform of the laws affecting women's inheritance and land rights.

Conclusion(s)

The first part of this paper has mapped the problem bedeviling women's inheritance and land rights. The second part followed by

---

[138] Presidential elections were recently held and a change of government has occurred while municipal, regional and Parliamentary elections are awaited by mid-2012. No other time could be more appropriate to made demands for legislative reforms that in the coming year.

examining the ways and means by which NGOs can contribute to gender-balancing reforms for better recognition and promotion of those rights as rights that hit the very core of women's dignity as human beings. It has also been demonstrated that there is urgent need to synchronize the activities of NGOs engaged in the fostering of women's inheritance and land rights.

The collaborative work carried out by the IDRC in partnership with the University of Buea has already laid the foundation for the opposite approach that brings all stakeholders into one agenda. At the level of execution however, tasks might have to be assigned in accordance with partners' capacities and geographic locations.

Transparency and accountability in NGOs is often compromised because of high levels of poverty and unemployment that has pushed many to create NGOs on hidden agendas for personal enrichment. In fact, NGOs serve more like catchment areas for soft foreign money rather than serve as accountable structures. By regrouping into networks, partnerships, consortiums, the NGOs become checks on one another and uplift their individual and collective dignity and performance(s).

Perspectives/Recommendation

With the outcomes of laid out hereinbefore it is recommended that the gender focused initiatives like IDRC-UB partnership project be expanded into other parts of Cameroon so that the ultimate proposals for reform will be informed by sensibilities from across Cameroon and not limited to the North West and South West Regions.

• There also needs to be an expansion of the stakeholders to include not just women's NGOs by other NGOs provided they are working for the promotion and protection of women's rights.

• Men should also be targeted so that the synergy from the traditional conflictual gender relationship on the matter should be transformed into a force towards positive and mutually beneficial results through the creation of equal access to rights to inherit and to own land by women and men alike.

- There has been ongoing work on a harmonized family Code. It is critical that NGOs network and lobby of inclusion in the Family Code provisions that will protect women's rights better than they are now.

- NGOs, can also campaign for a comprehensive review of the laws and regulations on land ownership rights and the procedures for effectuating them with affirmative and more protective provisions for women seeking to acquire legal ownership of land.

- The Agricultural and rural development Sector should mainstream women's land rights in their policies and projects in an affirmative manner.

Notes on Contributors

Florence Awasom nee Asaa is a Judge in Cameroon, and is currently the president of the court in Batibo. She is a very distinguished advocate for women's rights, especially on issues of Land and Inheritance. She serves on the Cameroon Heifer International Board of Directors and has been a two term member of the Heifer International Board in Little Rock Arkansas. She is involved in gender issues with many local and international Non-Governmental organizations. Mainstreaming Gender in the Development process is her passion. She holds a Bachelor's degree in English Private Law and Maitrise from the University of Yaounde; and a Postgraduate Diploma from the school of Magistracy (ENAM) Yaounde. Email: cnawasom@yahoo.com

Harmony Mbuton Bobga is a prominent Lawyer, Human Rights Crusader and Executive Director of the Human Right Centre, Bamenda. He is holder of LL.B. (Hons) (Calabar), B. L. (Lagos) Pg.Dl in Law (Yaounde), LL.M. (Nottingham, UK). Email: bobgambuton@yahoo.com

Michael Akomaye Yanou has a Ph.D. from Rhodes University, Grahamstown, South Africa and is a fellow of Wolfson College, Cambridge UK. His research in both institutions dealt with the conceptualisation of access to land as a human right. Before this, Dr Yanou received an LL. B (Hons) Calabar, LL.M (Nig) and a BL from the Nigerian Law School V/I Lagos. He is presently an Associate Professor of Law in the University of Buea, Cameroon and is involved in active legal practice as the managing consultant in Shalom Legal Consultants, Buea. He has written 4 books and over 15 articles in international journals. Email: yanoumn@yahoo.com

Irene Fokum Sama-Lang is an author of six articles. She received her LL.M in International and Commercial Law from the University of Buckingham, United Kingdom in 1992, she is awaiting to defend her PhD in Employment Security at the University of Buea, Cameroon, She is currently a Lecturer of Land Law amongst others at the University of Buea, Cameroon. Email: finds_1999@yahoo.com

Lawrence Fon Fombe is a senior lecturer in Urban Studies and Development Planning at the University of Buea Cameroon. He is interested in Digital Cartography as an important tool in managing spatial variations and environmental problems. He received a B.A and Doctorat de 3e Cycle in Geography from the University of Yaounde respectively in 1982 and 1989. He is a holder of a Ph.D. at the University of Buea Cameroon (2005) and is a member of the Association of American Geographers (AAG). He has published several articles in scientific journals and a book on the urbanization Process in Cameroon. Email: fombefon@yahoo.co.uk

Lotsmart N. Fonjong holds a Ph.D. in Human Geography from the University of Yaounde 1, Cameroon and an M.A. in Development Studies, from the University of Leeds in the United Kingdom. He is Associate Professor of Geography and currently Vice-Dean for Students' Affairs in the Faculty of Social and Management Sciences at the University of Buea, Cameroon where he lectures both in the Geography and Gender Studies programs. He is the author of seventeen scientific articles in international peers reviewed journals and of two books: *Transforming Rural Space through Non-governmental Efforts in North-western Cameroon*; and *The Challenges of Non-governmental Organizations in Anglophone Cameroon*, both published in the United States. He has won several international grants; been a visiting fellow to a number of universities in the United States; and belongs to several learned societies including ISA where he is a board member of the Research Committee on Environment and Society. His research interest is in Natural Resource Management, Women's Rights and Non-Governmental Organizations. He is currently studying for a Certificate in International Human Rights at the University of Cincinnati-Ohio, USA. Email lotsmart@yahoo.com

Ngwa Nebasina Emmanuel is the first holder of the Cameroonian *Doctorat D'Etat* degree in Geography. He is a full-fledged professor of Human Geography at the University of Yaounde I, Cameroon. Since 1975, Ngwa has been teaching, directing students' theses, and undertaking personal research for publication in journals. He is involved in consultancies, outstanding of which is his development and rendering operational of the notion of Village Community Development structures in the Bafut Fondom in North West Cameroon. He is the author of 3 books, a chapter contributor to many more, and has some 30 published scientific articles to his credit. He held the chair of the Geography Department from 2000 to 2005. Ngwa's current research interests are focused on the sustainable management of natural resources, gender and sex debates in environmental management, the sedentarization of (minority groups), the Mbororo- Fulani of North West Cameroon. Email: nebasina4@yahoo.co.uk

Patience Munge Sone holds an LL.M from Free State, Blomfontein and a Ph.D. from the University of Buea, Cameroon. She is currently a Lecturer in Law at the University of Buea, Cameroon

Vera Nkwate Ngassa has for the past twenty four years served in the Cameroon Judiciary alternately as a prosecutor and as a judge. She also teaches in the Department of women and Gender Studies, University of Buea. She is dedicated to advancing the rights of women and children. As a judicial activist, Vera broke new ground in the areas of women's property rights and spousal abuse. Part of her work is featured in the BBC International Award winning documentary "Sisters in Law." She is author of "Gender Approach in Court Actions ," "Gender Law Report ," "Custom the Woman's greatest yoke ," "The Common Law – An Endangered Species." Justice Ngassa holds a "License en Droit" from the University of Yaoundé and a Post Graduate in Magistracy from ENAM (National School of Administration and Magistracy) Yaounde, Cameroon. She

159

is presently an LLM Student at Georgetown University Washington DC USA. Email: verangassa@yahoo.com

TSS { Rebecca

G   A
F   B Dave
        C Jason?
    D Jason?
T & T
Mel

TS next

A
B
C
D
E

A   A
D   D
B   B
E   E
C   C

D

B

C

A   E
1st P S E

S 5, Sal less
P 6
Juna 3

I J K

I + K 1st

JK

4 1h   1pm
         salex

Production 1
HR   2
Sales   3
Engineering 4

S
R   never behind P or Q

1st P S E

2
U
Q
5th

P
U
R

Q

CPSIA information can be obtained at www.ICGtesting.com
Printed in the USA
BVOW030043260412

288707BV00001B/4/P

9 789956 726837